THE BOOK OF
ANGELS

DEDICATION

This book is dedicated to the journey in life that the angels call the Way of Love and Light, leading to wholeness and harmony. When you have realised that Love is Infinite and Light is Eternal, and that everything in the Universe, including your own Spirit, is woven with Love out of Light, then you have found the Way.

I hope this set of book and cards will bring you much happiness. My life certainly changed dramatically when I was 'highjacked' by the angels in 1999. Since then I have personally found inner peace through the Way of Love and Light. Use my *Book of Angels* and the *Guardian Angel Cards* to bring greater harmony into your life and to help you, too, to find the Way. Call on your angels and talk to them as often as you can - it will only bring joy in the angelic realms!

Remember, Love is the Key.

Sending you much Love and Light
Angela McGerr

Contents

Inviting angels into your life   4

Your guardian angel   5

How the book and cards work together   6

Invoking angels   8

Gold, silver and balance   10

Using the Guardian Angel Cards   14

A single-card message   14

A three-card message   15

A-Z of Angels   20

Grounding and balancing with the caduceus   122

A gold and silver meditation   124

Using colour and the chakra energy centres   126

Chakra affirmations with the angels   128

Working with Pistis Sophia   130

Using the power of Sacred Seven   133

Opening the heart to achieve universal harmony   134

Cross-reference of life needs and angels   136

Further reading   142

Acknowledgments   143

INVITING ANGELS INTO YOUR LIFE

The Book of Angels and the *Guardian Angel Cards* have been brought into being to allow the love of the angels to enrich your life. Angels are the messengers of the Creator - indeed, the word 'angel' comes from the Greek word *angelos*, meaning messenger. You could say that angels are the go-betweens or forces of energy that interact directly between the Creator and mankind. Some have called them 'the breath of God'. For most of us it is easier to relate to angels, whom we can picture, rather than to the Creator itself. That is as it should be, for the angels are there on behalf of the Creator to guide us by example with their unconditional and non-judgemental love, so that we can achieve our higher purpose in life.

All angels have a supervisory role in the world of mankind, though they cannot actually interfere in any way unless invited to assist. The key is that you have *free will*, and can choose whether or not to ask for aid at any time. Asking for angelic help does not mean that a situation you are going through will be removed, but you will be given loving comfort to go through it and emerge on the other side with some serenity. If invited into your life, angels, who are charged with overseeing everything that happens in this world, will help protect your spirit from being broken. Life contains periods of happiness and sadness, joy and grief. You will rejoice in the good times and the bad times will bruise you, but the only way you can learn wisdom and grow spiritually is through the balance gained from these experiences, which will lead gradually to understanding and maturity.

Life is all about the achievement of balance - between the physical and spiritual aspects of self, and between the masculine and feminine aspects of self. While your birth-assigned Guardian Angel provides general support and assistance, the Gold and Silver Guardian Angels specifically aid you with the balance, integration and harmony of all aspects of self.

YOUR GUARDIAN ANGEL

On your incarnation into this world, a Guardian Angel is assigned to you to give you loving support throughout your life. This special angel is charged with helping you to identify appropriate goals and grow in maturity and wisdom throughout your time on earth, so that you find inner peace.

If you are able to divine the name of your Guardian it facilitates calling upon this special angel. Although this can be difficult, there are ways of finding out the name. You may be told in a dream, or in a meditation. Or you could simply send love to your angel, ask and see if a name comes into your head. If this is the name of your Guardian Angel then this name will crop up (perhaps on the radio or TV or in a newspaper) two more times afterwards. Three is the number of dDivine Truth, so if you receive the same name three times it will be a name of spiritual significance.

In the same way that you have an assigned angel, everything in the universe has a Guardian Angel to aid the finding of true purpose. For example, there are Guardians appointed by the Creator for specific things such as the stars, the elements, for animals, trees, colours and so on; and also for all human life issues - problem solving, hope, creativity or self-development - in fact, for all aspects of your daily life. All these angels would be only too pleased to bring loving support to your life, or you can invoke them to help people or things you care for, bearing in mind that the angels work always for the highest good of all concerned.

The angels described above are known as the Gold and Silver Guardians, each of whom has a specific role in which they can bring you loving support. So long as your intent is honest and you are asking from your heart with love, you may call upon the power of these angels by name and receive the attendant gold or silver energy (see page 8 for how to invoke angels).

HOW THE BOOK AND CARDS WORK TOGETHER

The book and cards offer you three different ways of consulting the Gold and Silver Guardians, depending on your need at any one time. For an immediate angelic message, you can take one, two or three Guardian Angel Cards. If you have a specific situation that requires angelic help you can use the cross-reference section of the book (see page 136) to look up the angel you need. The third way is to work gradually on aspects of your life with all the angels in the book.

The Book of Angels

This book (a sort of angelic bible) contains an A-Z of over 100 named Gold or Silver Guardian Angels, each of whom gives you a personal message of support. This support is offered in conjunction with their special individual focus (assigned by the Creator). For example, if you look up Michael, Golden Guardian of Strength, Protection and Truth, under 'M', you will find that he helps you to work towards communicating and living your personal truth, and when you have done this you can move on to Absolute Truth.

You can read the book at any time, simply opening it at random, and gradually get to know the angels very well. The more you read and learn about angels, the more you will wish to invite them, and their unconditional love, into your daily life. The book will enable you to call on angels frequently by name for guidance and loving support in all sorts of different ways on a daily basis, thus enriching your life more and more on a long-term basis.

On page 136 you will find a cross-reference section, alphabetically arranged by life situations. So, if you need an angel for a particular matter that has arisen in your life just at this moment, you can look up the situation and the name of the angel in charge of this will be revealed. Taking the earlier example, if some aspect of truth became an issue, you could look up the word 'Truth' and find that the Guardian Angel assigned to this is Michael.

The Guardian Angel Cards
All the angels in the book also feature in the Guardian Angel Cards, as follows: 48 Golden Guardian cards; 48 Silver Guardian cards; 48 Key to Balance Cards. The purpose of these cards is to give you immediate information from an angel for your personal life guidance at any time.

You can choose to take one, two or three cards to receive your message and do this as often as you like. Each message, which is short, simple and direct, will be something the angel wishes to draw to your attention concerning your current life. If you then look up this angel in the book, the message will be further amplified.

For instance, you might choose a card whose message is *Michael: Speak and live your personal truth*. This might be all you need to know, because it will be a message that will relate directly to something that concerns you at this point in your life, but if you wanted to learn more then you could look up Michael in the book for a deeper insight and more information about this angel.

The Guardian Angels offer their gold or silver energy to help balance and harmonise you and your life. Apart from gradually learning their names and special roles, and becoming aware of how they can support your life, you may wish to know how to build further on this new information. Once you have determined the angel or angels you need, you can begin to invoke them at any time to bring you their special energy.

INVOKING ANGELS FROM YOUR HEART

Depending upon your situation at any one time, you will be guided towards certain Gold or Silver Guardians. To start inviting them into your life, you can invoke these angels in a special way in order to be able actually to feel their energy rays of pure, unconditional love. This may take a little practice, as you are developing a new, sixth sense within yourself, but please be patient - it will happen! Every time you do this invocation from a loving heart, your own energy vibration will rise infinitesimally as you grow closer to the angels; in due course you will feel their energy rays, which are composed of light and unconditional love.

You can invoke angels as often as needed , so long as you ask with an honest and loving intent. This is their role as given by the Creator and they can be in many locations at once, so don't feel selfish about doing this! To outline the basic philosophy:

- The ancient and sacred names of the angels (a prayer in themselves) carry a specific sound vibration.
- Three is the sacred number of manifestation of Divine Truth (for example, the Trinity).
- If you ask from your heart, they will always respond.

So, you start by calling the angel by name three times. You then ask the angel to bring you their special gold or silver energy vibration. Complete the invocation by saying the words *"In Love and Light"* three times, signifying that your intent is honest and comes from your heart. For example, to invoke Golden Guardian Raphael to help with golden energy you would say:

"Raphael, Raphael, Raphael, please bring me your golden energy; in Love and Light, Love and Light, Love and Light".

It helps to close your eyes to monitor the response of the angel, as this removes visual stimuli and you can concentrate more on what you feel. This might be tingling energy, warmth or a cool breeze on palms or fingers (usually starting in the left, or taking, hand), or around your heart. Sometimes it is felt in head or body, flowing down the arms or legs. Each angel will give you a slightly different response, rather like a signature, so that you will gradually get to know each of them. Afterwards, always send Love and Light to the angels in return.

Once you get to know the angels and their particular roles, you can invoke the angel whose help you need and ask them more specifically for help with this situation. You will be amazed how even the most difficult situation will become easier to bear once you feel you have the loving support of the angels. With the angels around, you are never alone.

GOLD, SILVER AND BALANCE

We all have both a masculine and feminine aspect to our personality. In this, we are divine reflections of the Creator, who is the perfect unity of these two opposite yet integrated aspects. You might say that the aspect of Father God is gold, linked with the sun, Raphael and warm energy; while that of Mother God is silver, the moon, Gabriel and cool energy. If you were to look at a cross with equal arms, this would represent the horizontal line, with balance being at the central point, which equates to your heart.

ACTIVE AND PASSIVE BALANCE

Your male, or gold, aspect is the part of the personality that operates the left brain. It is the organized, rational part of you that powers logical and analytical thought and directs your actions. Business people work mostly with their left brains. If this part of the brain is used in isolation the result will not always be completely successful.

The female, or silver, aspect operates the right side of the brain. This is your passive side, the part of you that feels and thinks deeply, and is sensitive and intuitive. In artistic and creative people the right brain generally dominates, and they tend to be less organized and regard situations from a different point of view totheir logical friends. Decisions directed solely by this part of the brain may also not be fully successful.

It is only when you balance and integrate both gold and silver aspects correctly that you begin to think and act as an individual with a rounded personality. In this mode you are much more likely to take the most appropriate action for your highest good, because you are combining both logical-analytical and intuitive-creative thought processes before making a decision. Because such decisions are taken from a balanced position, therefore, these more considered resulting actions are the ones that bring long-term happiness.

THE GOLDEN GUARDIAN ANGELS

The Golden Guardians help you with masculine, left-brain situations, for instance when you need to make a decision to take an action of a physical nature. All angels bring unconditional love - the Golden Guardians support your left brain with love in the form of golden energy. This aids logical and systematic thought processes, review of situations, ability to make informed decisions and take appropriate action over yourself or your life. At the same time, this takes into account your need to remain balanced in these situations if they are to be for your ultimate benefit.

THE SILVER GUARDIAN ANGELS

The Silver Guardians assist with silver matters, which are those of your feminine, right brain. This is where you need to use intuitive thought, considering matters in your heart as well as your head, analysing your feelings and instincts in the matter, but still with balance in mind. This applies also to your spiritual path. The loving silver energy these Guardians bring enables you to see yourself and your life in a slightly different way, perhaps rejecting action in favour of allowing certain situations to come about, for your maximum and highest good.

THE KEY TO BALANCE

What is important is that the balance is the right one *for you*, neither too much nor too little gold or silver, leading to the correct proportions of both masculine and feminine self, for the next part of the equation is the balance between physical and spiritual self. When the angels have guided you with their love to work towards gold and silver balance within mind and body, they will urge you towards gold and silver balance within spirit, to complete your life harmony.

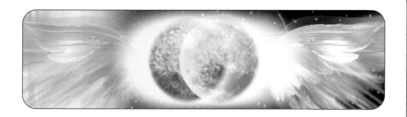

PHYSICAL AND SPIRITUAL BALANCE

As you start to work with the Gold and Silver Guardian angels and learn more about them, you will find another way of benefiting from their unconditional love and help in balancing your life.

A second way of regarding the gold/silver balance is that it can be specifically connected in terms of gold for your physical self and needs, and silver for your spiritual growth and direction. When looking at the equal-arm cross once again, this represents the upright line, with the balance at the heart centre. In this respect, some Guardians guide you in clarifying your physical values and goals, but at the same time help you to move along the spiritual path at an appropriate pace. This may be a slow process in your life at present, but you will still be moving forwards.

For example, Shekinah assists you with finding the right loving partner in your life who will support you as you continue on your spiritual quest, and Hermes Trismegistus offers his special path of spiritual wisdom. Among the Guardians are angels who wish to emphasize to you the importance of spiritual growth in your current life and offer you ways of pursuing your path. Primary among these, Metatron helps you to reach your own crown and open fully to spirituality, and Melchisadec offers his key to inner peace. Pistis Sophia tells you that your life template can be rewritten by the power of love. These three great angels offer their unconditional and loving energy to help you 'fast track' spiritually, if you so choose. As you accept their assistance, the colour vibrations you receive will rise and become more refined. Having worked through gold, silver and the normal rainbow colours, you will find that you are working with pale silver and pale gold, as well as the pastel colours of the spectrum. At this point, you may encounter the delicate pearl or opalescent colours of Love and Light.

By receiving guidance at the level you need, you will gradually attain a position of balance between the physical and spiritual self, leading you to a feeling of unity and harmony with all life. You will have moved through two stages: firstly, healing/integrating/balancing yourself as an individual; then, with angelic help, you will have applied this to your life and all those you care for. At this point the equal-arm cross will appear to be perfectly balanced through you both horizontally and vertically, with the centre point at your heart. In the final stage you will be working from this heart centre. You will wish to serve, for you will have the capability of channelling (receiving and passing on) the crystalline diamond ray of Seraphiel (unity of silver and gold with diamond white) for the benefit of helping to heal, harmonize and balance All Life.

USING THE GUARDIAN ANGEL CARDS

🪶 Each Gold Card contains a message from a Golden Guardian concerning an action or decision you are guided to take for your highest good.

🪶 Each Silver Card offers a Silver Guardian whose guidance on an intuitive level should corroborate your own decisions or inner thoughts/feelings.

🪶 Each Key Card offers further advice to aid your life balance and harmony in a unique and special way.

You can use the cards in many ways. The simplest is to spread them all out face down in a bowl. As you pass this bowl you can take at random one, two or three cards to receive a message and do this as often as you like, asking the Guardians to guide your selection for your highest good.

A SINGLE-CARD MESSAGE

You may be thinking about taking some kind of positive step, and are therefore drawn to pick up a Gold Card, as these feature active-principle messages from the Golden Guardians. The card you are drawn to will suggest a decision or action the angel feels you should consider taking at present, and the Guardian will offer golden energy to support you. The message should coincide in some way with your own thoughts, but of course you always have free will to decide whether or not to accept the angelic advice proffered.

Or you may have inner intuitive feelings about how your life is progressing that you would like to clarify; therefore you may be drawn to choose a Silver Card. The Silver Cards give passive-principle messages from the Silver Guardians. On this card the angel message will be about something you need to be considering or intuiting; once again this should help to resolve your own thoughts.

The final enabler is the third card - the Key Card. You could simply choose one of these to provide a Key for what to do next if you feel blocked in life for some reason. The message on this card will guide you on how or when to unblock whatever is causing you a problem, freeing you in some way so that you can move towards greater life balance.

A THREE-CARD MESSAGE

A more complete way of using the cards is to take one of each. You can consult them over a certain matter (or ask for general life guidance) and then allow yourself to be drawn to one Silver, one Gold and one Key card, whilst at the same time mentally asking the Guardians that the three cards you select will offer Divine Truth. Having chosen a gold message revealing an action, and a silver message for an intuitive solution, you may wonder how to follow up these messages. The Key Card provides the last part of your angelic guidance. With the Key Card you receive further advice and a focus on what to do next to attain the gold/silver balance that the cards suggest you need. Some of the Key Cards refer to a timescale for you to follow, some to a further action, and others suggest colours or tools for you to use to attain balance.

On the following pages, I show you some sample three-card readings. Though the message on each card itself is instant, you can obtain more information from the angel presenting on the card, and clarify or amplify your guidance, by consulting the angelic profiles that follow in the A-Z of angels. Here, you will find the angels' channelled messages. Try to absorb these into your heart, for when you start to live in your heart, rather than your head, you are truly moving towards unconditional love and therefore drawing nearer to the angels themselves.

Tual
Time to de-clutter and simplify your life

Tual's golden energy can bring positive changes into your life. Begin to simplify or de-clutter your life in order to clarify your position.

The Key is Spring to sow the seeds of a new life

The Key is to start sorting things out now, because Spring brings opportunities for you to start a new life leading to greater balance.

Geliel
Allow closure in a certain matter

You are guided to let something that has been ongoing in your life draw to a natural conclusion.

Dokiel
*Improve your work and
home balance*

*The Key is a more
harmonious future*

Ramiel
See things more clearly

This reading suggests that your life is currently out of balance in
terms of work and home, with either too much time at home or vice
versa. Dokiel suggests that you need to improve this balance to find
peace and harmony. Ramiel gives advice on how to see both your
current situation and, indeed, your life more clearly. The Key is: if
you can take immediate steps to start to rectify this then the angels
tell you that your future will be more harmonious than your present.

Hadakiel
Time to stop being judgemental

The Key is to forgive and heal the past

Cassiel
Find serenity once more

This message from Hadakiel urges you to stop judging yourself too harshly, as this means that you and also others will fall short of your expectations. Your action is to let go of judgement. By doing so, Cassiel explains that you will move towards serenity and peace. The Key is that it is your attitude in the past that is affecting you and that you need to focus on this and take steps to heal and forgive. This will free you to move forwards to find serenity.

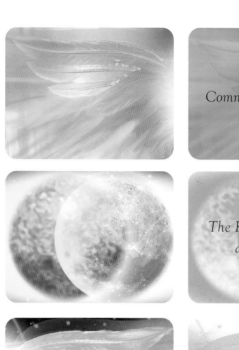

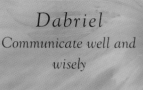

Dabriel
Communicate well and wisely

The Key is Wednesday and the truth

Adiel
Allow a certain situation to wind down

The message here is that there is a matter on which you need to communicate wisely; the angel Dabriel urges you to use written communication, for that will be more effective. Taking this action will allow a certain ongoing situation to wind down (Adiel, an angel of an appropriate moon phase, will assist). The angels suggest that the day to communicate is Wednesday; you must ensure that you focus very carefully on writing only the truth in order to sort out this situation.

A-Z of

ANGELS

Achaiah

Guardian Angel of the Secrets of Nature

I am found in the rich golden energy of nature's grace - her secrets of colour, fragrance and form. Mine is the beauty of the butterfly dancing in the sun, the bright and shining petals of the flowers, the divine symmetry of a shell.

Some of nature's secrets can be found in flowers. Brighten your day by instinctively choosing flowers of the particular shade that attracts you and bringing them into your home. Each colour carries a different vibration and these vibrations harmonize with the energy chakra system of your body. Each time you look at these flowers, you are absorbing not only their beauty but also their colour and symmetry into your system, helping to bring back equilibrium. You can also benefit from flower fragrances that enhance and delight. Perfumes such as rose and jasmine are especially linked to the angelic realm and serve to call angels to come closer to you. The scented oils distilled from my flowers can also help to heal your life in many ways. Rose helps to heal the heart, and lavender is relaxing and calming. These can be used on pulse points, chakra points, or to scent a room in an oil burner. Learn also the power of flower essences, for these are some of nature's secrets that help to heal and balance your life.

Nature's symmetry and proportions are pleasing to the eye. Consider the spirals that occur within shells: these spirals are repeated beneath the earth, in galaxies as well as in the DNA spiral within the cells of the body. The shapes and patterns of nature, and her divine blueprint, are echoed in mankind as well as the animal kingdom, so that to be in harmony with nature's secrets is to harmonize with all life, the greatest secret of all.

Adiel

Guardian Angel of the 14th Mansion of the Moon

I am the silver light that flows into your intuition, guiding your inner thoughts. My power starts at full moon; as the moon wanes you can start to wind down a situation in your life, freeing you to move towards your higher purpose.

The 28 Mansions of the Moon are the mystical days of the moon's journey through her phases, and each of these days has a place and relevance to mankind. The 28 days divide into four moon quarters of seven days each. I am the guardian of the third moon quarter, that is the day of full moon and the six following days - you may use my quarter to start to bring something to a conclusion, if this is for your highest good.

You may well already know that to which I refer, for in your heart you have pondered what to do about it. I urge you to make a timely decision so that during my moon phase I can help you with the loving determination to let change happen. Then, at the next full moon you can actually begin.

Do a meditation on the day of the full moon itself to boost your own intuition with moon power and silver guidance. Then start allowing the winding down of whatever it is - a project, situation or relationship within your life or work. With a loving heart, continue during my phase to follow your intuition and you will surely start to move towards the eventual closure that you seek.

Adnachiel

Guardian Angel of November and Sagittarius

Like the archer of my star sign, my golden arrow is ready to take your eye towards new and exciting horizons. I bring the marvellous possibility of expansion through vision and action, to make your dreams become reality.

I help you to bring about changes or enhancements to your person as well as your sphere of activities. With my assistance, new and far-reaching career opportunities can arise, perhaps even involving relocation or overseas travel. If you allow me to guide you towards spiritual growth, I will urge you towards researching new philosophies that will cause you to rethink your beliefs.

Invoke me now to help you open the first door to these new possibilities. First you must have a vision, for this enables you to focus your energy and will on a specific goal rather than just on a vague feeling of restlessness. You may already know where you want to be, but not how to get there. Or you may need to take some quiet time, or perhaps meditate, in order to receive guidance. Either way, let my golden energy assist you with clarity of vision and also with how to take the necessary and vital steps actually to bring about your self-development. Your higher purpose beckons, but what use is it to live only in visions, if you cannot move from concept to actuality?

There is much within you that awaits new direction. The call is coming, or has already done so, and you will start to move forwards, step by step until, after a while, the more interesting and focused 'you' you become will cease to be able to recognize the 'you' of your former life. Listen for my guidance, for it is time for you to start to fulfil your true destiny.

Ambriel

Guardian Angel of May and Gemini

*I offer my powerful silver energy to bolster your intuitive skills
in solving problems, wrapping you in bright silver rays to deflect
negativity from others. Listen to your heart, for the answers to
all you need to know will lie there.*

Through my sign of the heavenly twins, I bring you flexibility and
adaptability in daily life and work. Because of your quick brain
and sympathetic ear, you are often sought out for help and advice.
Sometimes, listening to very negative situations can drain your
energy, but you are loyal and find it hard to say no, for you know
that your listening skills do benefit others. In these cases I can
protect you by wrapping you in a cloak of silver rays, so that you
can counsel others but also deflect negative effects from yourself.
You give of yourself lovingly and loyally to others and it does not
go unnoticed by the angels.

At present you may have a problem of your own to solve,
possibly involving travel of some kind. Be open to the new
opportunities that are ahead - you can invoke me to guide you for
your highest good. Allow enough time in your busy life to deal with
your own problem! When you plunge into situations - for you are
enthusiastic and too ready to give your all - I urge you to hold a little
of yourself in reserve. Use silver energy to boost your intuition as
you resolve your own outstanding problem in the best way. But
before you make your decision, invoke my guidance and don't forget
to listen to your heart, for the answer will lie there - the past is
written but the future still holds many choices, some of which will
lead you to the Way of Love and Light.

Amnediel

Guardian Angel of the 7th Mansion of the Moon

I am the pure silver light that flows into your dreams to recharge your aspirations. My light builds gradually to the wondrous power of full moon, a time of fruition when your dreams can become reality, if for your highest good.

The 28 Mansions of the Moon are the mystical days of the moon's journey through all her phases, each having a place and relevance to mankind. The Mansions divide into moon quarters of seven days each - mine is the second moon quarter, that is the seven days leading directly to and including the day of the full moon. By developing and enhancing your intuition with the moon's silver rays you may use my quarter to help make something happen. These seven days are a time of bringing to fruition a project, situation or relationship within your life or work, so long as it is with a good intent. This may refer to something you have been working on for some time, but at the next full moon you can let this matter can reach its climax. You probably know very well the matter concerned, for you have wondered for a while how to progress it.

Make any decisions in good time, so that when it comes to my phase I can support you with my love. Your own intuition can be magnified to maximum potential by the love in your heart and the waxing power of the silver rays of the moon, culminating in full moon on the final day of my phase. Plan for the matter to come to fruition on that day. After this phase you will receive further angelic guidance, for this is but one step on the Way of Love and Light.

Anafiel

Guardian Angel of the Heavenly Key

I help you to find your own heavenly key, for my pure silver light shines on the path that shows you the way. The essence of all knowledge and truth - the very seed of life - is held in your own heart and is found by the power of love.

Firstly, I would counsel you that you should not spend all your time wondering about heaven, its mystery and how to get there; it is important to live your life in the present rather than only in the future. Instead you should focus on how to find a way to bring heaven to earth. When, with my loving support, you have perceived the way, you can instruct others and enable my message to be more widely disseminated.

This is what I wish to disclose. At present it is as if you stand before a very high wall. You cannot see what is beyond. Within the wall is the old and weathered door that leads to the garden of joy and contentment. The door is partially concealed with trailing plants, so that at first you do not even know that it is there, but gradually as you clear away this concealing growth you perceive this mysterious door. To open the door you must find your own personal key. With diligence and trust you will identify the key and, wonder of wonders, there will come the moment that you place your key in the ancient lock and turn it. The door swings open - and the most amazing thing of all is that as you look through the door everything is revealed as really so very simple.

You realize that all the time the knowledge you sought was actually to be found in the love within your own heart. This is spiritual knowledge, the wisdom that allows you to feel at peace and in unity with all around you - all of Creation. The mystery is that there is no mystery, the key to all that is heavenly is love.

Anahita

Guardian Angel of Medicinal Plants

It is my love that helps each plant to grow and flower, my wings that lift the seeds to spread and multiply the opportunities, and my silver energy that combines this power with the water of love and life to make a remedy.

Once man knew and understood my medicinal plants, processing their leaves or flowers to make healing infusions and oils. I rejoice because today this knowledge is being retrieved. In addition to this, my flowers of fruitfulness are being used in new ways made possible by the technology of your age, and therefore much healing work is taking place. It gladdens my heart, for the desire to help others out of compassionate love greatly aids our angelic work.

Perhaps you are one who once knew all these secrets, and had the skills of memory, hand and eye to apply them to help others. If so, then you will be ever drawn to the names and characteristics of my plants, for something in your soul will remember. You may not have understood before now why you had this fascination, but I tell you that if you seek to learn some of this vast area of knowledge, you will re-acquire your old intuitive skills. From deep within the well of knowledge you will draw your water of love and life. The information you learn will aid you firstly to self-heal, and then to help others, so if this resonates in your heart, begin your quest as soon as possible. Accept this role and surrender to faith and trust to unravel the ancient secrets of healing with plant energy vibrations. Then as you gradually gain confidence in your skills, and replenish your own intuitive reservoir of silver energy, you can draw on this once more to benefit others.

Ananchel

Guardian Angel of Grace and Acceptance

My loving and gentle silver energy enfolds you, assisting you with graceful acceptance of your present situation and reminding you that all things pass, wounds eventually heal, prayers will be answered and in time all will be well.

It is I who give you the grace to accept whatever life offers you, as well as the ability to be grateful for assistance from others, for giving and receiving compassionate and unselfish help is an important part of spiritual growth. Help may be offered to honour something which you have given to that person in turn, or it may be simply to offer a helping hand to you in a time of great need with no thought of return at all. However, how easy it sometimes is to have too much pride, and through this pride to reject others' help! If this resonates with you in any way, let go of a little of this pride, for those who love and care for you will feel joy at being able to help you through a difficult situation.

There is also the matter of acceptance of life's dramas, and the turn of fortune's wheel. Whatever you may be experiencing at this moment, in universal terms you must accept that it is as it should be. All is happening for a reason and, though this reason cannot always be perceived at the time, the higher purpose will be revealed in due course. Try to surrender with love, patience and trust - the more you can do this, the more you will gradually be shown. As your soul develops there are many karmic lessons to learn - some of which are hard indeed - and they are only learnt by experience. Knowledge plus experience becomes maturity, which can be used to guide others. Invoke my help if you feel bereft of fortune now, for I will comfort and enfold you with my silver rays until the good times return.

Aniel

Guardian Angel of Luck and Silver Protection

Perhaps you need me even at this moment, to bring luck or protection. I bring a cool stream of pure silver energy that flows completely around you at a time of need, wrapping you in a protective and shining silver cloak of light.

For good luck you can inscribe my name on a silver pendant or bracelet and wear this close to your heart, or you can write my name on a piece of paper and place it beneath your pillow. I may come to guide you in dreams - keep a pencil and paper beside your bed so that when you wake you can record my message before it is lost.

As well as guiding you at this time for your highest good, you can also invoke me to bring my loving protection to you. Close your eyes and call my name; then imagine a stream of pure, cool silver energy flowing around you in a clockwise direction, like a shimmering cloak made from coils of living light. Wrap it around yourself completely, with a hood over your head and face, and visualize the cloak reaching right down to the ground to cover your feet. Silver is the colour of invisibility, so wearing this cloak, or mentally placing it around someone else at a time of need, or in a hazardous situation, can also be very protective. This is my silver gift to you and those you love and care for in life.

Arad

Guardian Angel of Beliefs

My powerful silver energy flows to your soul, the individual core of you that helps shape your character and personality, that makes you the person you really are, for you are what you believe in and believe yourself to be.

There are many types of belief: self-belief, belief in those you love, spiritual belief, belief in a higher purpose to existence. Without these beliefs, would not your life be emptier and without real purpose?

Your own beliefs may be strong and constantly reassuring for you, but do not let them become too rigid - allow them to expand as you yourself grow and develop. Perhaps you sometimes struggle with self-doubt. If life is testing you, you may be in danger of losing your beliefs altogether. Invoke me to enfold you in my gentle but powerful silvery wings, to protect you with my love. I urge you to ensure this side of you is nurtured and cherished, for it is your spiritual cornerstone and underpins your existence.

You can liken your beliefs to a new gold or silver ring that you might wear. When you are young, like the ring your beliefs are shiny and unblemished, having never been tested by being exposed to the outside. It is easy to maintain beliefs when they have not been challenged. As life goes on, your ring becomes scratched and loses some of its patina; similarly, your beliefs become dented by experience. Beneath the scratches, however, the ring is still the same precious metal, and so it is with your personality. I help you to let experiences shape your character while ensuring they don't damage your integrity. Invoke my silver energy to surround your soul, protecting it during dark times, so that though your spirit may be bruised it will never be broken.

Aratron

Guardian Angel of Nature's Magic

See my mystery in the stars of the night sky, and their effect on the life of man. I reveal my powers in the beauty of silver raindrops on a spider's web, on the bark of a tree and in the haunting sound of the rhythm of drums.

Mine is the wonder of old wisdom known since ancient times for practical uses and healing benefits. I support you in using my natural medicine for positive changes in yourself and your life. The wonder of nature surrounds you always, though sometimes your vision is clouded by life's daily stresses. It is time to allow some of my soothing silver energy to flow into your body, to help bring about gentle relaxation.

The scientific discoveries of your age have brought great healing developments, but this does not negate all the old teachings that even now are being retrieved and followed once again. Apply your intuition to learn about my mysteries and use my magic - always with a loving intent - in order to help yourself and those around you.

Examine the ancient knowledge of medicine and shamanic traditions found within the indigenous peoples, knowledge that has been handed down for centuries, and find ways of using a little of this wisdom in your own life. Now is the moment to seek out what you need of the old, combining it where appropriate with the up-to-date offerings of nature's remedies, for this blending will become important in your life. If this resonates intuitively with your heart, invoking me will enable a gradual synchronicity to appear. I will lead you step by step in the direction you need, for nature seeks to weave this special silver thread of magic into your future.

Ariel

Guardian Angel of Earth and Air, and Pluto

I am the meeting of under world and over world. My silver and purple rays of magic pierce the veils between the two worlds, allowing the boundaries to be crossed and the ancient mysteries to be revealed to the seeker after Truth.

Mine is the love that aids you in understanding that all is not visible to the eye alone or audible to the ear - it is necessary to see with the heart and listen with the soul to learn of these wonders. But before you can see through the veil of mystery and illusion you must self-heal to find your heart centre. I bring you the special healing potential of earth and air to facilitate this process, which can be of particular benefit if you feel down or depressed. It is time to be reborn with the power of my elements.

Visualize yourself as a tiny plant in rich earth, the medium for your new growth. Any dark depressive energy within you is absorbed and you are cleansed of old patterns of behaviour as you surge towards the surface and the light. Feel the elements of water and fire also nurturing your growth. When you reach the surface, you are filled with the power of light. You grow and flower, and now as a tiny silver seed you are borne aloft into my air, where, scoured clean, you soar into the blue as if on invisible wings and are reborn in a beautiful rainbow arcing across the sky.

Use each rainbow colour to replenish your energy until you reach my indigo-purple ray, and then invoke my aid to breathe this in, to start opening your psychic senses when the time is right. Then you can begin your real life journey, for I will lead you through the veil to all worlds.

Barakiel 1

Guardian Angel of October and Scorpio

I am the golden force that helps you to calculate chance and risk, whether in people, ventures or situations, for I bring you positive energy and luck to power your thinking and help you determine your best way forward.

Consider your life to be like a game of cards - is it luck the way the cards will fall, or is it chance? Let's consider luck - do you feel lucky? If you do you will be a person who recognizes luck's unpredictability, and takes this into account, but also spots opportunity and maximizes it. Those who feel lucky constantly bring luck into their lives, but the reverse is also true, so manifest more luck by concentrating on a way of thinking and acting that is positive instead of negative.

Then there is chance; perhaps you can aid chance by calculating the odds, memorising which cards have already fallen, and thereby evaluating the possible outcome of the game. Applying this analogy to life, you can invoke me to help you by bringing positive golden energy to such calculations. This energy aids weighing and balancing risks and rewards involved in projects you are considering; you can then ask within your heart whether or not you should go ahead with that particular venture. Things may not always be what they seem; even so, I counsel you that some of these possible ventures contain lessons in life for you to learn, but you may still seek my aid as I guide you always for your highest good. Listen to and absorb my golden wisdom to underpin an important decision you are considering. Then you can either decide to go ahead, or let it go to seek a more appropriate alternative, one that is ultimately - as you will later discover - for your greater benefit.

Guardian Angel of February and Pisces

I offer you the silver protection of my loving energy. Your intelligence and thoughtfulness are qualities that others admire; I enfold you with my love to shield your sensitivity, for you are compassionate about people and causes.

With this message I offer you loving protection, for you are one who cares about many things. You are passionate about many causes, including protection of Mother Earth. You realize that the earth has suffered, and you find ways to help her to heal man's damage; I see this care, and support your work with my silver rays that combine strength with tender love. I guide your spiritual path to enhance this aspect of yourself, aiding you in dealing with past karmic issues to open up your way ahead.

Sometimes you care too deeply, for you have to live in this world, or you give too much of yourself unwisely - it is your loving compassion that influences this aspect of you. Invoke me to protect you at such times and to help you safely develop your psychic and intuitive powers, so that you can ask your heart which causes or people are worthy of your support. Here you need wise judgement.

Your sensitivity means you are often hurt, but it is this, coupled with an artistic ability that may not be fully utilized at present, that enables you to communicate at such a deep level with others. Let these latent skills come forth, with my loving support, to help you to comfort and aid others in coping with life's traumas, for you are also understanding and thoughtful. Be patient, for as these trials in turn allow your intuition and spirituality to develop further, at the appropriate time entirely new dimensions will open in your life.

Camael

Guardian of Tuesday, Mars and 5th Heaven

I am divine justice. I exemplify the golden force of courage that brings passion: for what you believe in, for gaining the utmost from opportunities, for life itself. My energy guides you to your personal empowerment of light.

On Tuesday, my day, focus on enhancing your energy and invoke me to help you succeed in your personal battles. My strong wings support you as you fight with integrity and vigour for your principles, for all you have achieved, and for those you love. If you do not have the courage to defend all you hold dear in life, in the end you may lose everything. To stand firm in what you believe to be a just cause is not easy - it takes determination, stamina and conviction. If this is your need at this time, then the power of my golden love will fill you with these qualities to help you accomplish your aim, because combining love with power makes for a radiant strength that will flow forth from you. In turn it will inspire others to action for justice.

I also join with you to re-affirm the foundations of your own earthly life, to make you strong and secure, especially if you have been through a period of change or instability that made you a little fearful of the future. Let my loving energy displace all this fear, and fill you instead with ruby red rays of courage and confidence. My love reaches out to guide you to build further on this, to energize, secure and strengthen your very roots and root chakra to make the firmest possible foundations in life. Then you will be empowered with love to go in whatever direction you choose to find your pathway of Love and Light.

Cambiel

Guardian Angel of January and Aquarius

Like the water carrier of my sign, I bring the silver water of life to flow into your heart, allowing your feelings to grow and develop to your full potential. For, above all, I urge you to listen to your own intuition and to follow your heart at this time.

I come to remind you of the importance of your ideals, principles and hopes, and to assist you in maintaining these - especially when you are tried and tested by life. You can be positive and capable, sometimes choosing to suppress some of your innermost feelings so that you can function satisfactorily in the day-to-day world - the world of decisions, logic and action. This is your gold, left-brain aspect. Within all people, however, resides the other self - your silver, right-brain aspect - that is dreamy, less practical and sensitive. Both aspects of self need to be in balance. Perhaps it is life itself that has persuaded you to lose sight of the importance of this, or it may be because of the nature of your relationships. Whatever the reason, I urge you to address your silver aspect by focusing more on your own intuition. My silver moon energy and water of life flow into your heart, aiding you to start to consider your decisions with both heart and head, for giving equal weight to both of these will lead to increased wellbeing.

As you gain the appropriate balance between your two aspects, your true individual personality emerges even more strongly. Your outlook will be more rounded, enabling greater understanding and sympathy for others. Then, as all your inner needs start to be addressed, you will become calmer and feel more fulfilled. This will lead to a sense of peace, and greater contentment with life.

Cassiel

Guardian of Saturday, Saturn and 7th Heaven

I pierce the darkness of the night with my glorious silver rays, pinpointing the eternal contrast of dark and light. All will encounter this contrast in life's journey, but I lead the Way to the pure silver light of peace and serenity.

I hold the Gate of 7th Heaven that can only be passed by those souls who accept the opposites or contrasts of life, and the need for reconciliation. It is I who help you to balance your life in terms of happiness and sadness, high points and, occasionally, despair. I come to comfort you at those times when life has seemed to be against you and bring you slowly back to peace and harmony, with the knowledge that when the hour seems darkest, light is nonetheless never far away.

Consider a bracelet made of individual links, shaded one link at a time from black to white. If you start at the black link, each next link grows paler, but when you get to the pure white link then the very next one is black! The contrast serves to emphasize the difference, and so it is with life. All lives contain some suffering, and this makes the times of happiness an even more precious gift to enjoy. To suffer is to learn understanding, sympathy and compassion - though often coupled with a desire to be alone. However, to be filled with joy is to want to share a little of this with others, touching lives like a sudden sunbeam on a wintry day.

If you have recently suffered grief or loss, you need not do so in solitude. In the dark and lonely night of the soul, when tears are near, mine is the loving comfort you can invoke to be with you and to lead you gradually back to serenity and the light of a new dawn.

Dabriel

Guardian Angel of Writing: Heavenly Scribe

It is my responsibility to record the story of your life - past, present and future. In flowing lines your past is written, but if its legacy lingers on in the heart it may not yet have its finishing touches; this affects the scripting of your future.

Just now I come to you to help you in resolving an issue, in which you need to master my art of written communication. An important aspect of the happiness of your future may depend on your present decisions and actions, for you need to write to someone. It is of utmost importance for this that you master the secret of the effective written word. Even more than your speech, what you write to others lives on in their minds and hearts and cannot be unwritten. Also, they may keep your words to read again and again.

If you are prepared to write your communication, mine is the unseen hand that guides you. I send my golden rays firstly to shape your thoughts and then to help you express them clearly, honestly and with integrity. As your need arises, invoke my aid to ensure your written words convey your meaning accurately, do not wound unnecessarily, and accomplish your purpose.

Though you cannot change your past, the power of words can convey your forgiveness or help you to atone for a past action, laying it finally to rest. Or perhaps your missive will simply bridge a gap that should never have been allowed to develop. Invoke me for the courage and determination to write your message, for by doing so you will allow yourself to move forwards in my warm golden glow so that I may record for you a brighter future.

Diniel

Guardian Angel of Luck and Golden Protection

I am with you when needed, bringing a stream of golden energy to create a bubble of bright and living light to envelop you with luck, healing and protection. Fill your heart also with my golden light to heal and help others.

You can inscribe my name on a golden pendant and wear this close to your heart, or you can write my name on a piece of paper and place it beneath your pillow. Invoke me at any time to bring my loving protection to you and guide you at this time for your highest good. If you have a friend who needs me, give them also my name, and suggest they call on me. Show them the Way of Love and Light by opening the first door to surrender and acceptance.

You can also invoke me to bring my unconditional love to you and guide you at this time for your highest good. For protection, close your eyes, call my name and then imagine a stream of pure golden energy flowing around you in an anti-clockwise direction, until you are completely enclosed in a bubble made of shining light. Remember also that gold is healing energy that you can harness for yourself. For example, draw this stream of living light into your heart, filling it with love and warmth and allowing hurt to be healed.

Then, when you feel ready, magnify this love as much as you can before sending it, with the power of your will, directly from your own heart to the hearts of those you love.

Dokiel

Guardian Angel of Work/Home Balance

I hold the golden scales that in this case contain your work and your home life, between which a delicate energy balance must be achieved if you are to feel things are harmonious, and also to find true peace of mind.

Your two worlds of work and home must peacefully co-exist and not be opposed or detrimental to one another. Are you spending too much time at work? On the one hand, I recognize that you want to be successful, that you need enough money to live, but what is enough? Have you perhaps let ambition carry you on until you have lost touch with the difference between wants and needs? Or is your ambition driven by an underlying desire not to be at home? Either way, this could mean your life is taking you away from a path of Love and Light.

Alternatively, you were born with many inherent talents, and with great potential. For your own reasons you may be wasting your days at home and not using your skills and abilities in the way they were intended. You may have failed to achieve your life purpose by hiding away from the world, perhaps because of lack of confidence, motivation, health or even for reasons of indolence.

Whichever way it is, I urge you to review your life without delay, for only you can make the decisions to correct the balance. Of course it is easier simply to carry on as before. But I remind you that if, deep down, you truly wish things to be different, you must face the reality of your situation. Then, with the loving support of my golden rays, pledge to take positive action towards a better future, one that is more harmonious, happier and more fulfilled.

Duma

Guardian Angel of Silence

From the void, the origin of all life, I sweep on my golden wings.
Mine is the medium of contemplation, the still and silent core of
your being wherein all is known but may not yet be understood.
I aid you to find this understanding.

If you are bombarded and swamped every day with noise,
information and potential knowledge until your brain either reels
with the cacophony or reaches saturation point, then I come to help
you. Without my golden silence you cannot fully process this data,
and I urge you to remember that without processing there is no way
of progressing.

During your life path you wish to learn and to achieve, so that
you can reach what you measure as a successful conclusion. How
will you know what you can reach, without silent meditation on your
ambitions? How will you even know when you have attained your
goals? If you take the time to pause and reflect, it may be that even
your goals themselves are changing. You may be successful as
measured by your personal criterion, but are you happy?

We angels ask you to ensure your criterion for personal success
contains both material and spiritual goals, for without this balance
there can be no inner harmony. Step back from the noise and
surround yourself completely with my golden silence so that for a
short time you can simply be, for if this message resonates within
you, it is the first step. Let me envelop you within my golden wings,
and give you rest within the heart of your heart where is found the
point of perfect, silent peace.

Eth

Guardian Angel of Time

I pour the golden stream of time from one chalice to another.
Back and forth I pour it for time is endless as it travels - present
into past, into future and back to past. The idea that time is
fixed is only a construct in the mind of mankind.

Time is not as constant as you may think! The past has different
qualities - sometimes sharp and clear as a photograph, sometimes
hazy as if viewed through a veil. Use your own powers to guide your
memories - the power of love to make them sharper or the power of
forgiveness to veil a little of that which you wish to forget. Time in
the present can also be flexible - how often have my hours seemed
endless to you on one day, but flown all too swiftly on the next? If
you wish to understand it better, take my time to allow your
consciousness to expand, with my assistance, for if you wish you can
embrace the fluidity of time and also space, to be in Unity with All.

    I can help you to bend time if your need is great, but I counsel
you not to use my magic frivolously. If you sincerely have a specific
need to make time last longer, invoke me from your heart, explaining
why you ask my help. Provided it is for your highest good, I will alter
the golden ebb and flow of my time stream to help you accomplish
your task. Use this assistance wisely and intelligently and in the
furtherance of good. My love helps you to manage your present
more effectively, so as the golden stream flows on to your future all
will be well at the proper time.

Farlas

Guardian Angel of Winter

My season is beautiful in its stark grandeur, for it is this that sets the scene for the promise of spring followed by the blooming of summer. In my season, life is not extinguished but merely dormant and awaiting the warmth of spring.

Even as the autumn leaves fall from the trees, the buds appear once more on the branches to lie in wait for the spring. During the winter they make little growth, but still they are there, holding the promise of new life; it is merely a time of transition, and it is the same for you. Perhaps you feel even at this moment that you are being held back in some way, because little seems to be happening in your life, but I assure you even the times of waiting are valuable and can be put to good use.

Cleansing and tidying should have been undertaken in autumn, ensuring all is well, so that after my season of rest the earth is ready for replanting in the new spring. This can also be applied to you and your life. Use my season to meditate and calmly reflect and, if necessary, to consider changes to the way you think and act. Be patient - use the quiet beauty and peace of winter to rest and recuperate and to let go of old dilemmas and behaviour patterns. Use your intuition to see where you have gone wrong in the past. Resolve to bury these issues by year's end. Then prepare for your spring so that it becomes a time of fertility - expansion within and without, of both ideas and activities. As the year turns, your mind will achieve the clarity it needs to prepare for change, development and abundance.

Gabriel

Guardian of the Moon, Monday and 1st Heaven

I come on a pure silver spiral that flows from Mother Earth to link with Moon, governor of your emotions and moods. I am the spiritual awakener who visits you in your dreams, bringing you fresh hope and new aspirations.

My task is to guide you to fulfil your hopes and dreams, deal with your karmic issues and progress on the path towards harmony with All. This requires a balance between the active side of you - issues you decide and corresponding actions you take - and the passive side of you - things that you feel, intuit and think. Raphael and the sun govern your active, gold aspect, but it is I who care for the passive side of your personality with my silver moon rays, and encourage you to balance your actions with your intuition.

You may invoke my loving silver guidance in meditation, especially on Mondays, my special day, or when my moon is visible. Breathe in my silver ray; imagine drawing it through your feet in a clockwise direction from Mother Earth, and allowing it to spiral through your energy centres and into your heart. When your heart is full, absorb it into the cells of your body, feel the silver rays dissolve barriers you erected within to prevent hurt, sense your inner self and intuitive skills expand, feel emotional balance being attained. Let the energy spiral on towards your right brow, where it joins its silver radiance with the golden energy of Raphael to harmonize your masculine/feminine aspects and engender peace. If you work at this you can gradually attain the physical and spiritual wholeness you deserve, that is the first step on the Way of Love and Light. Then, if you so choose, I will lead you further, with brand new aspirations, on my shining silver path.

Gazardiel

Guardian Angel of the Rising/Setting Sun

Mine is the golden energy of the sun's daily path as ordained by the Creator, without which mother earth would be frozen and lifeless, for it is the light of the sun itself that sustains all the physical aspects of the earthly kingdom.

Have you ever noticed how the quality of sunlight is ever-changing - sometimes subtle and sometimes dazzling? No two sunrises or sunsets will ever be quite the same, for the radiance of the sun and interplay with the clouds is infinitely variable, moving and beautiful.

You too have a solar energy centre: the solar chakra centre of yourself is behind your solar plexus. This important area contains the full potential force of your will and mind, though this is often held back by trapped emotional turbulence which will also be within this area. Bring in the power of the sun to empower you by practising a sun meditation, whatever the weather outside. Invoke my aid and I will help you to breathe in love and golden energy to your solar plexus. Then, with the power of your will and intention, visualize this whole area of your body becoming bright gold as you ignite the sun within your own solar chakra. As sun energy fills you with vigour, it empowers your will to succeed in your chosen ventures, provided they are for your highest good. You can also send the energy throughout your body to dissolve hurt and heal all energy centres, and even down through your feet into mother earth, which will ground you as well as helping to heal the destruction continually caused to her by the greed of mankind.

By taking this step, you can choose to ask angels to activate your will and mind gradually towards spiritual progress and life enhancement.

Geniel

Guardian Angel of the 1st Mansion of the Moon

My silver light flows into your heart to guide your aspirations and fuel your intuition, to give you the power of knowing what you need to do. Make something new happen in your life that will be for your highest good.

I am a Guardian of the Mansions of the Moon. The 28 Mansions of the Moon are the mystical 28 days of the moon's journey through her phases, from new moon to full moon and back to new moon. The 28 days also divide into moon quarters of seven days each. I am Guardian of the first moon quarter, that is the day of the new moon and the six following days. You may use my seven days to bring about change and transformation, as well as developing and enhancing your intuition with the moon's silver rays.

   My moon quarter is a time of development, a window to allow a brand new project to start within your life or work. At the day of the next new moon, therefore, I urge you to follow your intuition to determine what you would like to happen, ensuring in your heart that you are doing this for the highest good of all concerned. It may be that you have already considered such a project, for you know in your heart that it is time to make something new commence. As the moon waxes ever brighter over the six days following the new moon, so you can absorb the increasing silver energy to develop further your intuitive powers. During this period I will help you with the courage actually to allow this project to commence. Then, if you follow your enhanced intuition and surround and bolster your plan with love, it cannot fail to be achievable.

Geliel

Guardian Angel of the 21st Mansion of the Moon

I am the silver light that guides you to know in your innermost heart that something must finish. Use my Mansion of the Moon wisely to effect closure of a situation so that you may move on to a new and different phase of life.

I am a Guardian Angel of the Mansions of the Moon. The 28 mystical days of the moon's journey through her phases are called Mansions, and each of these days has a relevance to daily life. The 28 days divide into moon quarters of seven days each. I am Guardian of the fourth and final phase of the moon's journey, the seven days prior to the silver sliver of the new moon.

This is the time of completion or closure, when you finally lay a matter to rest. It will be something directly relating to you - either a project, a plan that you have been carrying out, or a relationship either at home or at work that you know needs to be ended. This is your opportunity, and you can invoke me to bring you loving support provided that what you desire is for your highest good. You may have been wondering how to extricate yourself or to conclude this outstanding matter. I urge you not to delay further, but to use my particular and special moon phase to carry out your action. Ask me to guide you, in your heart, as to whether the proposed conclusion is right, and how to follow it through sensitively and thoughtfully. According to what your heart tells you, follow this intuition and use the power of love and silver energy on the six days before the new moon to effect closure. As you reach the day of the new moon, it is time to start a brand new phase in your life.

Hadakiel

Guardian Angel of Judgement

I show you my golden scales of justice, but ask you not to confuse justice with judgement. I teach you greater understanding of non-judgemental love that leads to expansion of your soul and brings you closer to the angels.

I come to guide you at this time, for the balance of your life can be affected by being too judgemental in some circumstances.

Firstly, consider how you feel about yourself and your life achievements. You must not judge yourself too harshly. If you set yourself standards that are impossible to attain, then you are forever doomed to disappointment. Why allow the negative energy of disappointment to surround you, for this will also affect others in your life. You will judge others - even loved ones - by the same exacting standards and they, too, will be found wanting. Real love tries not to judge but accepts frailty and failings. To be human is to be imperfect, but to work towards self-improvement and above all to be compassionate.

Review your goals and standards before it is too late, and allow for the possibility of failure. When things go wrong you have an opportunity to examine the reasons, to feel humility and then to learn from your mistakes. Do not dwell on these mistakes, but instead allow yourself to review them in a positive light, converting challenge to opportunity. Let this then guide you towards greater understanding of how failures occur and compassion for those involved - including yourself. By this means you will gradually let go of your judgemental attitude, feeling instead sympathy and empathy for all. In turn, this greater understanding leads to expansion of your soul; this is the golden path of unconditional love that, as you move on to it, will bring you ever closer to the angels.

Hagith

Guardian Angel of Metals

Mine is the ancient knowledge of metals, a gift from Mother Earth. I guide you with creative inspiration in working with my metals, and the power they carry when linked with the Sacred Seven planets of the solar system.

It may be that you are one who can actually work metal, bringing creative inspiration forth to make objects of beauty. If so, I come to help your creativity so that it flows from your soul and into the metal, from where it will reach and resonate with the souls of others. Also, I guide you specifically with those seven metals linked to the ancient wisdom of the Sacred Seven planets of your solar system, and thus in turn to the aid of the Sacred Seven angels:

🖎 Monday's ruler is Gabriel. Wear my silver or platinum on your left hand, to balance your feminine aspect and guide your intuition.

🖎 Tuesday's ruler is Camael and iron for courage and confidence.

🖎 Wednesday's ruler is Michael. Use my mercury as in a mirror, asking to see reflected your personal truth.

🖎 Thursday's ruler is Zadkiel. My metal is tin, more commonly found in the alloy pewter with lead. Use a tin or pewter bowl to aid in attracting abundance.

🖎 Friday is the day of Haniel and copper containing power of love; wear or use a piece of copper to guide your loving thoughts.

🖎 Saturday is the day of Cassiel; my metal is lead, once again found mainly in pewter. Use this to promote harmonious thoughts.

🖎 Sunday's ruler is Raphael, with a focus on healing. Wear my metal of gold on the right hand to balance your masculine aspect and to use the power of this metal for healing.

Hahlii

Guardian Angel of Colours

Mine are the rainbow colours and shades of Creation, mixed on a silver palette to enrich and heal your life. Each of these has a unique and special role, but when they come together they form the pure white light of Unity.

Make your life a kaleidoscope, for colour offers infinite possibilities for you to heal, develop and work towards balance. The Creator gave us, his angels, 12 colours of Creation. However, mankind is not yet aware of all these colours, for although the first seven (the rainbow colours) are clearly visible to you, the other five are perceived more through non-visual senses. For example, magenta, which is between violet and red, is the eighth colour and is for the higher heart chakra of unconditional love (the personal heart being green). It is more felt in the heart than seen with the eye. Of these eight colours, four - red, orange, yellow and green - are masculine, while four - blue, purple, violet and magenta - are feminine.

These colours are directly linked to your main chakra energy centres which, if functioning correctly at both physical and emotional levels, mean health and wellbeing, so healing and balancing each colour is very important. Each of my colours has many shades and you will be intuitively drawn to those you need. There are many ways of absorbing colour; you can invoke me to help you channel a specific colour in a meditation, or do a daily affirmation to focus on your need. You could wear it, or choose appropriate crystals or oils. Most people start with deeper shades, gradually working towards paler tones which are the higher vibrations. This is my Rainbow Path of Love and Light that takes you ever nearer to your goal: the pure, sparkling white that signifies Unity and spiritual connection.

Hamaliel

Guardian Angel of August and Virgo

I am the golden summer of your life as I bring my rays of infinite love to enhance or untangle relationships; my energy smoothes your life path, allowing you to move forward towards relaxation, tranquillity and harmony.

I come to assist you to enhance interactive skills both at home and at work, to help your day-to-day relationships. You have a natural ability with communication and I help you to meet as many new people as possible, for this develops your character and personality. Some relationships will work better than others, but all will teach you something and this is the road to maturity and wisdom. You also have intelligence and patience, spending much time in planning every detail of a situation, which is excellent, but do not lose sight of the fact that it is the doing and not the planning that is really important.

Also, you tend to worry, which is wasteful of your beautiful compassionate energy. It is this loving energy that makes you caring and concerned about others, but in danger of leaving too little time for yourself and your own life progress. Remember that if you are not allowing yourself the opportunity to rest or to develop this will gradually affect your relationships with others, causing you yet more concern that can even affect your health. Let me come to your aid - enabling you to operate more effectively. There is much to be done at present by those such as yourself who are filled with a desire to help others. I am here to help you nurture old relationships and meet new people as the golden flow of activity carries you forward. In the synergy of love, as you assist them they will aid your own evolution on the Path of Light.

Haniel

Guardian of Friday, Venus and 3rd Heaven

My message is one of Love and Light, purely and simply, for that is all you need. While infinite love heals, light eternally binds the universe with rainbow filaments, allowing my rays of emerald and magenta to unfold your heart.

I teach you the power of love in all its many aspects; my golden love and emerald/magenta rays begin the process of healing and opening fully your heart, allowing you to recognize the beauty in all creation, so that your heart flowers with true unselfish love and compassion. Do not worry if the contemplation of beauty moves you to tears - this is simply the sublime breath of angels communing directly with your heart.

I offer you the light in my pink mirror of love in order to see yourself more clearly. If you look in this mirror and practise using your heart as well as your eyes, you will learn to be able to see your true self - a beautiful being who is a reflection of All Life as created. When you can love yourself unconditionally then you can start to love others, faults and all, seeing the beauty in all things, for you have let go of judgement and found true compassion.

Let yourself surrender to love and beauty, and allow me to fill your heart with my warm and golden ray. This will overflow into your surroundings, helping those around you also to be healed and fulfilled, for love can transcend and heal all situations. The power of compassionate love transmutes negative energy, converting it into the positive vibrations that will attract new people into your aura. Allow light to prevail and love to flower in and around your life and nothing is impossible, for this is the key to All.

Hariel

Guardian Angel of Tame Animals

Mine are the creatures that bring such joy to your life. My message is one of grateful thanks, for as you love and care for my innocent ones, through doing so you draw ever closer to me, for all life is sacred.

I see your actions and I am with you as you help those who are helpless and rejoice in their company. How uncomplicated they seem compared with mankind; life would be simpler if people were to act more as pets do - without judgement, with acceptance, giving unconditional love.

Your love of animals will lead to guidance from them. If it has not already happened, a pet will come into your life to bring about expansion of your spirit. These are animals with ancient souls who come to teach and develop their human owners. Often it is because you feel closer to your pet than to other humans, and this a valuable means of learning a lesson of life and then progressing onwards.

On occasion, when the lesson has been taught and learnt, the animal will either pass over, or disappear. Much as you will grieve over this, you must let go of the animal whose mission has been accomplished and release its dear soul. When the time is right for your next learning experience, then another animal is likely to appear and a new lesson will begin. Your kindness and gentleness may be coupled with sensitivity and it is this that causes many of your hurts and upsets. Your animals will help to heal you and will try to bring you into contact with the right people, those of a like mind, who will respect your personality and respond gently and favourably to it, thus helping to shape your future.

Haurvatat

Guardian Angel of Rivers

I guide the silver river of your life to flow smoothly and free from too many rapids. Sometimes it is swift with strong current, sometimes there is a point of stillness where it hardly moves and all is revealed to you in startling clarity.

Consider yourself in terms of your river of life. At this very moment are you contending with the current, or are you hardly moving at all and wondering what to do next? Remember, such moments are given to you to use wisely, so you can rest from the current to view your way ahead. In the abundant river of life you also contend with both drought and flood, for it is never consistent, and during these periods you try to protect the life within and around you. Be comforted, for the wild rides allow you to sense the contrast, and who would enjoy a long cool drink if they had never gone thirsty? I help to protect you from the excesses both within and outside yourself, guiding you to channel your passion for life and live in beneficial rather than destructive ways.

There is also an ebb and flow with my tidal rivers - a time to go forward, which you generally prefer doing, and a time to hold back, when it would be your wisest choice. I ask you now to go more with both ebb and flow around you, for that is your smoothest course. Do not try to fight against everything, for this will take all your energy and avail you nothing - let the life force of my river direct you when to move and when to pause. Like my rivers, you have great power: use it intuitively when the time is right, always with love and not simply for personal gain, if you would find and keep inner peace.

Hermes Trismegistus

Guardian Angel of Spiritual Alchemy

My alchemy frees you from the physical and into the spiritual quest, for I am the 'thrice-great master of masters' and mine is the master key that unlocks the ancient mysteries. I aid the seeker of wisdom and ultimate truth.

These are my seven principles that you must labour to understand:

🌿 As we are part of the Universal Mind (the All), All is likewise part of us. Everything that is in the universe is also found within your heart.

🌿 What is in the world we inhabit (the world below) is an exact counterpart of what is in the world beyond (the world above) and the reverse is also true.

🌿 Everything, including mind, body and spirit, is composed of energy and in vibration at all times: the higher the vibration, the closer it is to the All.

🌿 Always there is action and reaction, for this is the natural rhythm of life. To understand or realize the one is to understand and accept the other.

🌿 Everything is dual, and has a pair of opposites that must be reconciled. In this reconciliation is the first balance to be found.

🌿 In the game of life you must learn that for every cause there is an effect. When this is grasped then the second balance is achieved.

🌿 There is a masculine and a feminine principle that must be harmonized in all. When this balance is attained, then is found Unity with All.

If you would follow these principles, then take the time to meditate upon each one, for as I have recorded in my book of philosophy, *The Kybalion*: "The lips of wisdom are closed except to the ears of understanding".

Iadiel

Guardian Angel for Dispelling Worry

My wings have the power to lift you from all thought of earthly care for one brief, fleeting moment. I suspend you in time and space like a great bird traversing a limitless sky, so that you can see your situation more clearly.

I am called 'the hand of God', and I bring my supportive silver energy to aid you with a certain matter. There is something you have been mentally wrestling with and worrying about, which fills your thoughts and consumes your dreams with anxiety. I come to urge you not to waste your precious time and emotional resources in this way, for you cannot directly resolve this issue - others are involved and must also contribute. They have been given free will to choose their ways for themselves; in the name of experience, they must learn their lessons in the school of life. Instead, I advise you to make a resolution to stand back and resolve to send love and light to this matter, whatever it may be, and to invoke me to support you in this determination. There is an ancient saying from when civilization was young: "And this, too, shall pass away". Negative thinking simply undermines; I urge you to send as many loving and positive thoughts as possible to a person, or indeed any situation, where there are difficulties. It takes a little time, but gradually, as with all things, a solution will be found.

If you are worrying on your own account, trust in my help as I place the hand of God in your own hand, and lift you in my wings to give perspective to your problem. I bring the silver strength of love and light to flow around this matter, and if you are patient all shall be resolved.

Icabel

Guardian Angel of Fidelity

*I give you my unconditional love without judgement or reserve
and remain unswerving to you in my loyalty, whatever you do or
say; this is my shining example: persevere in the spirit of love
and never betray your heart.*

I counsel you in loyalty and faithfulness to lovers, friends and family,
for this is the way of the open heart. How difficult it can sometimes
be, however, for it may be tested almost beyond endurance. I urge
you to maintain your loyalty to those you love for as long as you
possibly can. But if you have been betrayed in a relationship that has
gone wrong and you intuitively feel it is time to cut the ties, do so
with my silver energy. Ask three times in my name to be released
with silver rays of love, for as this severs ties that bind it also heals
and contains forgiveness.

 Be true also to the cause you espouse, for if you feel it is worth
your time, then it is certainly also worth your loyalty. Do not admit
the possibility of failure to yourself, but pledge the utmost energy
to success. If by chance it does not succeed, then learn a lesson and
grow wiser, but let it not be because of your lack of commitment
or broken promises.

 I urge you also to be faithful and true to your beliefs, which
shape your personality and, though they may be tested, do not let
them be destroyed, because they are a part of yourself which may be
lost for ever. If you are, or are considering, committing your loyalty
to work with the angels, then trust in the outcome. Surrender to our
love and guidance and we will lift your soul, taking you gently on
your spiritual path towards the light.

Isiaiel

Guardian Angel of the Future

On rays as fine as golden thread I weave the fabric of your future. To that end I come to guide your present, for it is the key to the pattern for regaining your contentment. Together, let us create a bright and harmonious tapestry.

If your past has been turbulent, I urge you not to waste precious time on recrimination; try to feel forgiveness rather than guilt about the outcomes. Others' choices, made through free will, were also to blame, and you must not shoulder all their burdens - they have their own lessons to learn. Moreover, if happiness defines your past and discord your present, it is of no use to spend your days on regrets, for this is a negative way of thinking. You know in your heart that my advice to you is wise.

However it was, you must place your past behind you, for by taking command of the present you can influence your future. I come to you in unconditional love, which helps to heal all situations, and I urge you to accept my assistance and follow my example. As you let go of emotional blocks over past issues - whether caused by guilt or deep regret - allow my warm golden rays of love to flow into you, bolstering up your inner feelings and confidence; with the power of your will, send energy back in time to heal the past. Then let this wonderful energy also surround you completely in an invisible yet protective aura of gold. By feeling and being positive once again you will create a more dynamic atmosphere, gradually attracting more of the same energy towards you - new people, situations and opportunities for abundance. Overall, this will present you with the prospect of a more balanced and harmonious future.

Isda

Guardian Angel of Food and Nourishment

*I bring my subtle energy into the food you eat to power your
physical health, but if you would seek true wholeness, do not
neglect your soul and your spiritual path in life, for this brings
harmony of mind, body and spirit.*

It is I who come to you to persuade you to consider all three aspects
of your health and work towards their balance. On the matter of
your body, I urge you to review your eating habits, ensuring that you
eat wisely and take enough exercise. Respect your body and treat it
as you would a dear friend, kindly and carefully and without abuse.
If you find this difficult, invoke me to help you to love and cherish
your body, for without a sound vessel how can you live life to the
full? If you do feel depleted and tired, your nutrition needs
immediate attention. A suitable diet, sufficient exercise - and if
necessary, specialist advice - will soon help to engender a feeling of
greater wellbeing. Do not expect others to do the work for you, for
it is you who must take ownership of your diet and health.

Feed your mind with new challenges, which energize and develop
your potential. Do not allow boredom to rule! Enrol on a course or
join a club to meet new people. My loving support helps you to take
these steps and encourages you to set yourself new goals - remember
that the prize is your future happiness.

To take the final step to wholeness, invoke my silver guidance to
find appropriate spiritual direction, for to balance mind and body is
but two parts of the triple equation and you must also nourish the
third part - your spirit - in order to attain inner harmony.

Israfel

Guardian Angel of Poetry

Mine is the silver energy that creates the living beauty and harmony of words, for a line of verse has powers of healing and can express innermost sorrows and feelings in a way that resonates with many others at the soul level.

Inspired poetry can guide you to understand why you have similar feelings trapped within and allow you to release these feelings, enabling you to find new joy. It can also make you laugh out loud, which is very beneficial. Perhaps you need poetry to lift your heart or soul once again. If so, seek a book of poems in a library or bookshop, invoking me to guide your choice, and you will be sure to come across something appropriate to restore your balance.

If you are gifted with the ability to write poetry, allow this creativity to flow. Few are those who can heal others by pouring their heart into words whose very passion seems to ignite the page on which they are written. Do not hide such skill away. I urge you to give your creation to the world to aid those who have not your gift of expression. In offering this loving help from the heart you also aid yourself immeasurably, for it returns to you manifold.

You can also see your life as a kind of poem, where you work towards feeling in harmony with all life. The power and magic of your words resonates through your soul and this resonance corresponds with the souls of others. In turn this power flows through the universe in a sublime harmonic pattern, in the same way as music and colour. If poetry is your gift, use it intuitively to help create and maintain this universal harmony so that it becomes your personal contribution to the unified consciousness of All.

Ithuriel

Guardian Angel of Your True Self

If invoked from the heart, I show you the person that you really want to be but perhaps have imprisoned for the moment. It is time to release your inner self from behind the bars you have erected, and embrace Truth and freedom.

Why is the real you behind bars of your own creation? Have circumstances placed them around you, temporarily or permanently, or have you simply ceased to follow the guidance of your heart?

The path of your life can be viewed as a glorious crystal mountain, at its summit the golden crown of your real aspiration - inner peace. Each face of the mountain reflects all that is best in you. Catch a glimpse of your reflection and marvel at your true potential, one in which absolutely anything is possible. At present, however, you may be imprisoned at the foot of this mountain and gazing towards the summit, feeling trapped in life. My golden energy dissolves the prison bars and shows you a route to follow. To be sure, it may not be an easy climb, but I urge you to start your ascent, for you do have the ability to reach your summit. All it takes is enough determination to break out of the prison you have constructed around yourself, and take the first step upwards towards real happiness and contentment. The higher you climb, the easier it gets to feel trust, love and acceptance of whatever lies ahead.

When you reach the golden crown of inner peace, place it upon your head and give thanks for the journey. As you wear the crown and look down from the summit you will see that, far from being the complicated situation you anticipated, like true greatness it is all very simple indeed.

Jofiel

Guardian Angel of Jobs and Roles

Everything in this world is in the charge of an angel, and happens for a purpose, although you sometimes only perceive this purpose in retrospect.

Look beyond the obvious to understand the current lesson you have been given to learn. The wisdom, protection and luck I bring are to guide you in finding the right job or role in life. Perhaps you are feeling unhappy or uncomfortable in your present position, whether at home or at work. However, I ask that you take the time to consider what you are learning from this role, remembering that often what you dislike in others is but a reflection of what you are yourself. Give the situation a little more time, with as much grace as possible. My loving energy helps your acceptance for just a while longer, for soon new prospects will arise for you.

Start to make something happen. Place my name somewhere nearby so that you can see it daily, and ask me to bring my golden energy to you, to guide and focus your thoughts and steps towards a brand new opportunity. Try to be patient, for there may be several different options about to present themselves to you, so you will have to choose from among them. Invoke me then to bring loving support, aiding you to make the right choice, the one that is for your highest good. As you take up this next challenge with energy and enthusiasm, my love will flow in and around you to add to your self-confidence. You will put what you have learnt in the past to good effect and grow in experience and wisdom as you work towards your real or higher life purpose.

Kadmiel

Guardian Angel of Good Fortune

At times of need (perhaps even now) you may invoke my loving assistance to bring yourself or a loved one golden energy for luck, healing and even protection. My gleaming energy flows around and through you, sent by love.

To keep my name always in your mind, you could inscribe it upon a golden disc and wear this close to your heart or on a bracelet. Alternatively, you can write my name on a piece of paper and place it beneath your pillow. Invoke me at any time to bring my loving protection to you or a loved one and to guide your decisions and actions for your highest good.

To help someone at any time, in any place, you can hold out your hands and ask me to place within them an imaginary bowl full of liquid golden light energy. This is for good luck, protection and healing. Using the power of the love in your own heart, visualize the person as a tiny figure standing within this bowl and see the golden energy flowing around this figure. As the level of golden liquid rises, let them be completely immersed in golden light. Then let the liquid drain away again, as if you have pulled out the plug in the bowl. When the figure is visible once again, see it surrounded with a glowing golden aura. Ask me to assist you in sealing in this good fortune and protection, in the name of Love and Light.

Machidiel

Guardian Angel of March and Aries

My golden energy guides your heart in decision-making, to influence your goals, for you may feel you completely understand your heart's desire, but it may in fact be your head's desire and will really not gladden your heart at all.

I guide mankind particularly in my month of March, but also generally during the period between January and March. I stress the importance of this time for you to make changes in your life, to bring about divine balance. You may invoke my help in achieving your goals, and I urge you not to be too impetuous or stubborn! Be willing to be guided. Think carefully and clearly on your life at present, reviewing exactly where you are. What is it that you seek? What do you feel will fulfil your dreams and make your heart full to overflowing?

You have much energy for living, and like the ram of my sign, much strength and determination to achieve your chosen goals. You apply this passion to all aspects of your life, but remember that you must also take the necessary time to think things through, to ensure that this energy is not misdirected. How often have you achieved your objective before, only to find that what you hold in your hands somehow disappoints?

During my special guardianship I support you in identifying what is the future that will benefit you most, to bring love and light into your life, and help you to direct your skills and resources accordingly. This change and renewal will include urging you to seek balance between mind, body and spirit. When you can understand the importance of all three elements in life you are truly on the path to inner harmony.

Manakel

Guardian Angel of Dolphins and Whales

My graceful and gentle creatures, whose origins are far older than mankind, are the voice of the sea herself, birthplace of life on earth. They have much to teach you, for they hold ancient knowledge from the dawn of your time.

Only now are you rediscovering this ancient knowledge and special power that resides with my sea mammals, a power that interweaves science and technology with their deep wisdom. When these strands are brought together much healing is possible, especially when interaction takes place between man and my beautiful creatures. This can be life enhancing in many ways, or even life changing. Listen to the haunting aeons-old sounds of my whales and dolphins. They communicate in unique ways, helping to heal the vibrations of the energy centres of your body. Also they give you inner spiritual strength in order to allow your soul to expand and develop.

Communing with dolphins, especially in their natural habitat of the oceans, helps to bring about energy balance within the mind, harmonizing both hemispheres of the brain and soothing those for whom life seems especially dark or difficult. Indeed, there are those who, having listened to the sounds of dolphins or whales, feel their lives are changed for all time in a deeply spiritual way. It may be an experience that would greatly benefit you - ask you heart to tell you whether the gentle and intuitive healing energy of my loving creatures can help you to achieve harmony of self and oneness with the All.

Matriel

Guardian Angel of Rain

I am the silver shower that sustains rainforest and desert. My rain also mingles with your sadness and sorrow, blending my drops with your tears so that they are absorbed and cleansed away, allowing recovery from hurt.

I bring the showers that fall upon Mother Earth to allow all to root and flourish at the proper time; even in her driest deserts do I bring life, for without me nothing grows or reaches fruition. If your life at this point burgeons like my rainforests then rejoice, for I shall aid your personal expansion, in the name of love, to maximize your time of plenty.

Each of my drops of rain reflects your life back to you; as you view it more clearly with my help, is it what you would wish? Is there something you need to overcome? Most people have suffered hurt at some point in life. If your heart is even now recovering from hurt, this can close it to new possibilities. With the gentle rain of tears from heaven I offer you the chance metaphorically to wash clean your life and re-open your heart. Let my silver tears flow in until your heart heals and expands like a flower with its promise of new life. When you feel cleansed and revitalized, go into your heart and ask yourself what you really want to do, or be, or achieve. No matter what you seem to have in material terms, what does your intuition tell you?

If any aspect of your own present resembles a desert, it too can be transformed with my love, with new ideas and opportunities - for love is the key to All. It is one of the most powerful forces in the universe, but if your heart is closed then you can neither bestow nor receive this precious gift.

Metatron

Twin Guardian of the Tree of Life

Mine is the dazzling silver-white ray, shining as the radiant light of crown. This is the summit of the Tree of Life, the divine connection that links All Life in universal harmony and the sanctuary of the pure white dove of peace.

I guide your spiritual direction through the allegory of the Tree of Life. You journey from the base of the tree (presided over by my twin angel, Shekinah) back towards the very top and crown. Both base and summit are your points of connection to the Creator and All Life.

All is possible for you in this life, which is or will become (if you will allow it) deeply spiritual. In your journey to crown perhaps you have not progressed very far as yet. If this is the case do not worry, for I am here to support you and, at the right time, to show you your direction. On the other hand, you may be deeply into your spiritual development. Whichever applies to you, all is perfect at this point and in accordance with the divine plan. Let your spirituality gradually become supremely important, for as you reach crown you grasp the secret wisdom of All. With this understanding you will be able to live in your heart and to achieve, maintain and deepen your divine connection.

As Shekinah helps you to secure your foundations in the earthly kingdom, I support and guide you from my place at the crown of the tree. From there it is but a flight with the white dove of peace to universal harmony. Then, as you continue to grow spiritually, reconnecting with All Life through sacred geometry, you will send and receive Love and Light, magnifying it within your heart for the benefit of All Life.

Melchisadec

Guardian Angel of Peace and Spirituality

Mine is the violet ray that transmutes illusion, lighting the labyrinthine way to your heart centre. I hold the chalice of life and the key; your quest is to find my rainbow path to the centre of the labyrinth, place of supreme inner peace.

I guide the journey of your life, and counsel you that this should be a spiritual progression as much as a physical one. To facilitate your spiritual quest, use rainbows in your life in as many ways as possible, for they will commune with your subconscious and engender even greater development. First, heal mind, body and spirit with rainbow colours, working through the normal spectrum as your journey commences until they combine into pure white light - this is the start of unity with All. Then, as you advance further on the spiritual path, you will find that each colour you work with becomes paler, more refined, and finally opalescent and pearly - these are my higher vibrations of the colours. I ask you to magnify these in your heart before sending them out to All Life. They will return to you manifold, bringing you ever closer to the angels.

Take the time also to explore fully the mystery of my own violet ray, for this magical ray has many shades, all of which transmute negative energy back to pure light, and it can be used at many levels both within and without. Invite this colour into your life daily to cleanse mind, body and spirit. Both violet and purple are deeply spiritual colours and intensify your route towards understanding different dimensional realities - other worlds that you may not see but will experience through other psychic senses. Travel through the veils of illusion with me as you move through sacred geometry towards the wonder of spiritual fulfilment.

Michael

Guardian of Wednesday, Mercury and 4th Heaven

From the wellsprings of light on a dazzling beam of gold I travel to strengthen and protect you; my brilliance dispels all darkness and falsehood from your life. My golden sword lights your way to truth, wisdom and freedom.

As lord of light and ruler of Mercury my primary gift to you is communication and truth. I ease all manner of dialogue you engage in with others, whether at work or at home. You have but to invoke my assistance for me to bring my blue energy rays to build your confidence and power of speech.

My further gifts of patience and calmness support you to find the appropriate time, as well as helping with the words you choose. I urge you to say what you really think and feel, perhaps for the first time, in the cause of speaking your personal truth. Then, together, we can open up your path of light. Aided by my loving strength, you can also take the difficult step of hearing and accepting the truth about yourself, and move from there towards living a more honest and fulfilled life, a life that lets go of pretence and pretension.

You can invoke me to bring my golden sword, to cut away things within your life you wish to be rid of, so long as you act always with integrity and do not use it to harm others. As I remind you, the gold energy of my sword of light may only be used in the cause of light. Use it to remove old behaviour patterns, or cut away insecurity from within, allowing you full power of self-expression. Then you can move towards the Creator's Divine Truth: this is the path of wisdom towards freedom.

Mumiah

Guardian Angel of Energy and Wellbeing

Imagine you are a vessel of crystal and can draw in my liquid golden rays of energy and wellbeing from Source itself, until you are filled to the brim with sparkling golden light, as together we cleanse, purify and balance your body.

I come to assist you, for there is a need for you to re-energize your body. Perhaps you have been ill, or life has drained you in some way; whatever the cause, you may feel physically depleted. It is time to rebalance your energies. I ask you to envisage your body as a vessel made of pure crystalline light, which is currently empty and needs to be refilled.

Invoke me from your heart, for your highest good, to bring my pale gold rays of energy and wellbeing, which flow like liquid light. I am with you to guide your thoughts, actions and expectations as you start to breathe deeply and rhythmically. As you do this, visualize pale gold rays pouring from above down into your crown and then cascading into the crystal vessel that represents the hidden structure of your physical self. As you imagine the liquid light flowing in, see the level rising in the vessel, until you are filled to the brim with tingling golden energy. If you will it to do so, this light will then overflow around you, surrounding you completely with a protective aura. Ask me to help you seal in the energy with the power of love.

Do this exercise as often as you can until you feel your passion for life being rekindled, and then pledge your newly found energy to maintain your improved health with balanced nutrition and a moderate lifestyle. As you attain a position of greater wellbeing you can address other important aspects of your life, seeking out your own path towards greater contentment.

Muriel

Guardian Angel of Cancer and June

I am the silver voice of your heart, rising pure and clear from your innermost sanctum to express your feelings, for you do not always let them be heard. In such self-expression I will aid you to find your empowerment for the future.

I come to guide you in issues of hearth and home and particularly to aid your contentment. Think of the peace you enjoy when surrounded by your own belongings and the people you love. However, at times - perhaps even now - an issue develops with which you are not comfortable, and you suppress your true feelings or pretend to agree, rather than being honest. This means that part of you is living a lie, but others think this lie is your reality, so you are creating an illusion around yourself. Ask yourself if you really wish to be living within such an illusion. These key issues probably threaten harmonious relationships, and I urge you to invoke me to guide your thoughts and decisions in this matter, for nothing will be resolved by your silence or by dissembling. Difficult as it is, and much as you dislike speaking out, now is the time to do so and to be completely honest. If you do not, matters will slowly worsen, resolution will be harder, and you will worry and deplete your precious energy.

With my loving silver energy to boost your confidence, try to formulate tactful and calm words in order to speak your heart's truth. If your loved ones or friends hold you in the respect you deserve they will hear and accept your point of view. It is important for your own future that you tackle this issue, for afterwards you will feel a marvellous sense of release and empowerment.

Mupiel

Guardian Angel for Mending a Broken Heart

Your heart is a beautiful flower, like a lotus or water lily. As I send clear green water of life to flow in to soothe and heal personal hurt, see the bright pink flower of unconditional love unfold, glowing in golden rays of my creation.

I come in unconditional love and support to those whose heart is wounded or closed and who feel that love has let them down. If you have ended a loving relationship and are broken-hearted, I help you to heal and re-open your heart. I do not judge you, for you may choose whom to love or with whom to share a home, but if on the scales of life you are unhappy more than you are happy, then review your situation. I ask you to remember that it is always easier to stay and hope things will improve, rather than take positive action and make difficult changes.

Perhaps you have created a hard shell around your heart, to protect it from further hurt. However, this also affects its functioning, and one thing is clear: it will prevent you from re-opening your heart to a new loving partner. Invoke me to aid you in healing your heart of past hurt. I stand before you with my wings of love around your heart. Breathe in my golden rays and allow them to permeate the heart itself. Feel the warmth of these rays gently dissolving away your pain and your protective shell. Then visualize emerald water of love and life flowing in to balance and replenish. See your heart like the bud of a water lily; give inner permission for it to re-open to love, and then imagine it unfolding into a beautiful pink flower. When your heart is filled with love, you are closer in vibration to the angels, because it is love that makes and maintains the vital connection.

Nadiel

Guardian Angel of December and Capricorn

I come to you on bright loving rays of gold, building your self esteem. I bolster this with further dynamic energy, bringing you the crystal power of vision and the chance to fly on my golden wings towards a clearer, brighter future.

Like the goat of my sign you are strong and determined, and a little stubborn - slow to give up doing what you have always done and cautious to venture into unknown waters without the certainty of a safe shore, but perhaps you are no longer fully satisfied. My love brings you the golden vision to look beyond the now to find real happiness, even if it means moving house, town or country to do so. My gold builds your self-esteem, for at times this has been threatened by occasional wrong decisions. You must put these behind you and, if you are living as you are only through habit, have the confidence to plan a more challenging future. I aid you with the thoroughness to think through and carry out your resolve towards dramatic changes.

Start soon, for time passes and you cannot go back and do things differently! If you define your past by periods of greyness and boredom, do not incur more regrets over your present. There is, or will be, an opportunity to do something completely different. When this choice comes forward, think very carefully about your inner feelings and sense of fulfilment. This is your chance to change direction towards a new life. Invoke my help with your decision. Your head may tell you that it is too late, or you are too old or set in your ways, but what does your heart say? If you really want to, you can metamorphose into someone completely different, travelling down a brand new avenue in life beneath my golden wings of love.

Nathaniel

Guardian Angel of Passion

I am the golden fire of passion, ignited within you once again and burning brightly. Like the phoenix reborn from the sacred flame, emerge triumphant from the power of inner fire to seek new challenges or horizons in your life.

When opportunity knocks for you, and the possibility of great achievement is presented, seek my guidance, for do you not wish to live your life passionately and succeed in your ventures? You have immense capability, although in the past you may not always have applied this in the best way. Sometimes your efforts have been misplaced, making you wary of committing yourself again, but it is now time to let your joy of life come back to the fore, to live your life to the full. In your heart you are aware that it is not really possible to gain much without commensurate effort. But you do have the reserves of vitality and enthusiasm to take advantage of a new opportunity. Even if it does not go entirely to plan, then still you will learn from it and grow with the experience, for it is this that brings maturity and power of discernment. You are born on this earth to live a life rich in such experience, to enjoy it wherever possible but also to learn appropriate lessons.

Let my golden passion rekindle your fire and power your efforts. Then, like the phoenix reborn from the sacred flame, emerge triumphant from the ashes of your past and seek new challenges, being thankful every day for your gifts - most of all for the gift of love. Your enthusiasm will be contagious and you will gradually light the fire of passion in others so that they too can be rejuvenated. As they in turn move on to new challenges, the fire you ignited will never be extinguished.

Och

Guardian Angel of Crystal Alchemy

From deep within Mother Earth I come with my crystal power, created when your world was young. For millions of years has my energy grown and developed; in the name of light I offer you now this power of alchemy.

I guide you in the use of the minerals of Mother Earth to bring about change and self-development within and around you. A whole world of knowledge resides within these minerals, and with this message you may harness the alchemy of my crystal energy to transform your life. Start with the crystals that correspond with the energy centres of your body, for they can assist you to correct imbalances and attain better health. Each of these is identified with a rainbow colour that holds a certain vibration. The energy can be increased with a corresponding crystal, which you can hold while doing a meditation, or making an affirmation.

- Ruby, garnet or red agate for root or base chakra.
- Orange carnelian, topaz or amber: the sacral chakra.
- Citrine, clear quartz or sunstone for the solar chakra.
- Emerald, tourmaline or rose quartz for the two heart chakras.
- Sapphire, blue topaz or lapis lazuli for the throat chakra.
- Amethyst, sugilite or sodalite for the third eye.
- Diamond or clear quartz for the crown.

To bring more of this wisdom into your daily life you can research the more advanced chakra healing, involving power stones such as selenite, celestite and angelite, calcite, hematite, kyanite, alexandrite and kunzite. This in turn is but a step on the way to such knowledge, intuitive powers and wisdom of which you have not yet dreamed.

Ofaniel

Guardian Angel of the Wheel of the Moon

Seek my help to draw the full silver power of the moon into your mind, where the pure light reflects to you your true purpose. Let this be a life-enhancing experience that you will build upon as a major step to universal harmony.

I am the angel of the moon's stately journey (the 28 days or Mansions of the Moon) as she sails through your skies. It is not only her beauty that you must recognize, for she is in partnership with earth. The power of the moon affects the moods of mankind, and her silver light is the source of intuition and the means of balance of the feminine aspect in both male and female genders.

The most powerful day is that of the full moon, when you may seek to absorb this silver energy to help achieve balance and to clarify your higher purpose.

If you would use this power, light a silver or white candle. Do this meditation at night, bathed in the moon's pure radiance if possible. If not, visualize the clear, silver light within your mind. Sit quietly and invoke me to surround and protect you with my love.

Breathe deeply to draw the glorious radiance of the full moon into your crown, allowing silver to fill your mind and deepen your spiritual connection to the universe. Ask for your intuition to be developed as much as possible at this time, and to attain true balance of your feminine and masculine aspects. Will this balance to be reached at third eye, and then at heart level. Allow the energy to flow down into your body, sending it through your legs and feet and into mother earth to heal and help to balance her - she will return this energy to you magnified with love.

Oriel

Guardian Angel of Destiny

*See in your mind a pair of magnificently wrought golden gates -
what lies behind? These are the gates of your destiny and I am
the angel who calls you from within; when I open this gate will
you walk through or walk past?*

I ask these questions, for I come to help you find your true destiny in
this life. It does not matter whether you are old or young, for destiny
can call you at any age. You may have spent many years engaged in
what you thought was a career or life calling, only to find that
suddenly you receive my wake up call which holds a promise to
change your life completely.

   Always you are given the choice on what to do, for you were
created with free will. If, when my call comes, you need my loving
guidance, invoke me then and meditate upon whether or not you
will accept this message and proceed to fulfil your destiny from that
point onwards. It may not be comfortable to change your present
situation or embark on a new career - indeed it may be a very great
challenge indeed, perhaps involving making personal sacrifices or
fundamentally changing your value system or way of life.
Considerable courage may be needed to follow this call to your
higher purpose, but if you decide to do so, embrace your destiny
with vigour and energy. If it feels right in your heart and brings a
warm golden glow that lifts your spirit, you may be sure that it is
your true path that now beckons. This is the path that you chose
before your soul descended to this planet to be born, so heed my
call with love and trust. I will open the gate of destiny to your path
of golden Light.

Padiel

Guardian Angel of Luck and Silver Protection

I am a silver angel of love and good luck, who comes to you at times of need. I teach you the radiant power of silver for, when combined with love, it brings healing and protection to you and those for whom you care.

At times of need you may invoke my assistance to help guide your thoughts and protect you with unconditional love. If you wish to keep my name close to you, you could inscribe it upon a silver pendant and wear this every day, if possible close to your heart. Alternatively, you can write my name on a piece of paper and place it beneath your pillow.

You may also invoke my help for someone else who needs it. At any time, in any place, you can hold out your hands and ask me to place within them a powerful yet invisible silver energy ball of good luck and protection. Visualize this ball as being the size of a football - you may actually feel the tingling energy. With the love in your own heart, ask to magnify the energy contained in this ball as much as you possibly can. Next, imagine the person you want to help as a tiny figure in the centre of the space between your hands. Then, with the power of your will, send the silver energy to this person by gradually closing your hands, until they reach the prayer position. As you do so say the words *"I send this silver energy in love, peace and light, love, power and wisdom, and by the greatest of these which is love"*. At that moment, when it is as if you are holding the tiny figure closely between your two palms, the energy will flow into that person, providing them with healing and protection.

Pagiel

Guardian Angel of the Heart's Desire

*My loving energy flows around you in a bright stream of gold -
allow this stream to carry you forwards, at your own pace, with
surrender and trust, as it conveys you gradually ever nearer
towards your true heart's desire.*

I bring love and support to help you fulfil your innermost dreams.
Do you have such a dream? If so, it is time to get to work on your
journey to make this happen! The road to your prize is an experience
in itself, for once you have focused on your goal, and if you are ready
to commit heart and soul to the venture, things will start to happen.
They will occur because you are sending positive energy to your
commitment. You may need to have patience, for at first it may seem
as if little is happening, but step by step I will help you. You will be
invited to attend something, or you will meet a new person. Perhaps
you will sign up to a course, or find an interesting book. All these
synchronicities are part of the plan, because the journey is just as
important as the destination itself.

Along the way your dream may even become modified - this
does not matter at all, because your hope, expectation and vitality,
the qualities that are empowering you for your journey, are also
developing and changing you. What does matter is that you are
moving forwards, with energy and focus, towards what you regard
as beautiful and desirable, and that your spirit is engaged in the
enterprise. How exciting it is to be one hundred per cent involved
in achieving your dream, in making this dream a reality. Let my
unconditional love be your guide, and be flexible and open as things
unfold, for with love as your motivator all things become possible.

Parasiel

Guardian Angel of Hidden Treasure

I am the shimmering silver light that shines from deep within you, the treasure of your true talents and abilities that you may have buried. All knowledge is held in your own heart and soul, and can be re-found with the power of love.

I counsel you now to find your own hidden worth. If you would find it, take a moment to try to think with your heart. Set your mind to one side, and use your intuition to feel what you are capable of. Perhaps life has conditioned you to think that you do not have hidden talents and depths, but I assure you that you have much to do yet in life and many skills with which to do it!

Remember your dreams of old - there is still all to play for! Breathe in my silver energy to bring self-confidence. Place my name up in your home, and invoke me daily to help you find your hidden talents. Little by little I will bring my energy of synchronicity to you that will clarify your path. Step by step I will guide you on this path, until at some point in the not-too-distant future you will look back to see how you have progressed. The shining treasure that was buried within will have emerged. Opportunities will have arisen to allow it to develop new experiences for you. Experience is the prize, for it leads to wisdom, and that brings a sense of acceptance and wholeness into your life. When your heart realizes and accepts this wholeness and how life changing it is, your ability will never again be hidden, nor will you let it be taken away from you. And so in some ways the cycle is completed, but your spirit will have grown immeasurably from it.

Pedael

Guardian Angel of Deliverance

I am the pure gold of unconditional love; my role is to help you to let go of a certain situation, object or person, for the time has come to sever the ties with loving intent, using the power of Love and Light, and not to look back.

There are many ways in which you might seek deliverance. Perhaps you are in an intolerable situation with regard to work, home or a relationship and don't know how to extricate yourself, especially if there are implications for others. Invoke my name with loving intent and ask for guidance on how to become free, without hurting others any more than necessary. You will be aided by sending Love and Light daily to the problem, which gradually moves things towards the correct solution.

You may have recently lost a loved one, leaving you with such a profound sense of bereavement that you feel as if a part of you has also died. However, in the name of love I urge you not to cling on to this soul but to let it go, so the soul can move on and you can slowly begin to recover. In such cases you can ask me to help you to release this soul into the light, with your love and blessing. Sit quietly, holding a photograph of the loved one, and imagine that a shining golden pyramid of my light is around and above you, with the point immediately above your head. Now, in your heart, say goodbye; breathe in my golden rays until you feel you are filled with this beautiful healing energy. Invoke me then, with the power of love and your own heart. Request that I escort the soul of the loved one - you may see it depart through the apex of the pyramid and upwards to the light.

Phaleg

Guardian Angel for Managing/Refocusing Anger

Mine is the golden power to help manage your emotions, to refocus the forces of energy such as anger or bitterness, freeing you from negativity to direct your passionate feelings in new ways towards a positive and dynamic future.

You have powerful emotions, but these can be either positive or negative. When positively directed, the force of your emotions can be very beneficial and, because you pour your very soul into what you do, can lead to great accomplishments. If it is a case of injustice and you are trying to right a wrong, then I come to support you fully at these times. However, when your head powers negative emotions such as unreasonable anger or hatred it can be misplaced.

I help you to manage and deal with this more destructive kind of emotion, which may be trapped within you because of past circumstances, constricting your soul. You can liken it to tentacles wrapped around your lower body, ever keeping your lower self locked in and, by closing the bridge of the heart to Love and Light, preventing the spiritual growth and expansion that you deserve. Invoke me to help you find a way of releasing or refocusing this negativity, leaving you free to move on in life. As I send you unconditional love in golden waves of energy, breathe it into your heart, soothing and calming your feelings. Then let it flow to your solar plexus, where harmful emotions may be trapped. Let the warm golden rays unwrap the tentacles and dissolve them away completely, mentally pledging that you will not allow them ever to return. You should actually feel lighter in spirit after this exercise.

Phanuel

Guardian Angel of Atonement and Forgiveness

I am the golden one who oversees all unkind acts done by mankind. Many are they who think that such acts are secret, but I see all, even as I offer you unconditional love. As I rejoice in kindness to others, I weep over cruelties.

In your past there is something that needs addressing, and I am here to help you overcome it. If it is something you have done to hurt another, then I urge you to make amends - it is never too late to ask for forgiveness. Perhaps you never meant to hurt, but the effect may linger even now. You may still feel guilty, in which case you must also forgive yourself, because to be human is to be imperfect, but to strive for improvement. Through me seek repentance, for this is the first step towards expansion of the soul towards the light.

But if you have been the victim of cruelty, then I bring my infinite love to be absorbed in your heart for as long as you need it. Invoke me every day to surround you with my golden wings, to support you as you weep, turning your tears into the water of healing and life. You cannot make the perpetrator ask to be forgiven, but through the power of love you can work towards forgiving that person, freeing yourself from the cycle of pain, resentment or even hatred that cripples your soul and holds you, too, back from the path to the light. Let my golden ray flow into your heart and soul, gradually dissolving hatred or bitterness into forgiveness, and despair into hope for the future. I send radiant light into your cells to heal also at this level, and seal in the healing for you, as my love guides you from yesterday to a more joyful tomorrow.

Phuel

Guardian Angel of Neptune and Waters of Earth

Mine are the powers that rule the moon's tides and all silver waters of earth, governing your moods and through this your daily existence. My water of life soothes and balances all emotions, bringing utmost tranquillity and peace.

If you would understand my powers, imagine yourself as my element - water in all her guises, water of love and life. Close your eyes and invoke my protection, surrounding yourself with my silver, deep emerald and turquoise rays. Imagine you are walking towards a beautiful sunlit scene of nature, with a still pool of water that reflects the heavens in its depths. Step into this water, submerging yourself fully if you can, and feel my element flowing right into your flesh, bones and blood, dissolving your cells so that you become one with me for a short while.

Be the medium that nurtures the fish and the gently waving water plants in the crystalline and tranquil depths. Above you, sense the rippling, sparkling but diffused sunlight. All is stillness in this pool, but travel further along a stream and feel the power of a waterfall as it descends to the sea. Join the fish in the currents of my sea and feel the racing waves and blue-green spume; sense the mysterious deeps. You are a haven for the sea birds and mammals, and within your soul you hear and understand their strange calls, sharing their ancient knowledge. This is the birthplace of the ancestors of man and through this ocean of knowledge you can let yourself be reborn with your mind, body and spirit - even your cells - washed clean and pure. Your heart can be healed with my water of life, allowing it to open and flower with compassion and unconditional love.

Pistis Sophia

Guardian Angel of Wisdom and Faith,
Heavenly and Earthly Mother

*I am veiled in celestial star fire, the light of the constellations,
for I, with my ancient wisdom, emanate from the Source of life
itself. My feet rest upon earth, within the sacred flame through
which you are born and sustained.*

I come to help you with new faith, for you can rise above adversity
and achieve your expectations and more. Like all humans you have
strengths and weaknesses - I help to strengthen these strengths even
more, and understand and forgive your frailties. Though you must
accept some setbacks as hard lessons that you have had to learn, they
also bring you the maturity that comes with experience. To build on
this, I bring you wisdom and spiritual sustenance to guide you.

Through me you can reconnect yourself to earth, and to the
stars, creating a pure energy channel. Open the meridian from your
crown chakra right down to base chakra. Invoke me to bring my
sacred energies in gold and silver rays of infinite love and
compassion, and I connect your crown to the stars with celestial
star fire and the base of your spine to earth with earth flame. As
you breathe in these energies, they meet and integrate in your heart.
Absorb the life-transforming rays into your very cells; as they begin
to heal you can regenerate your self-belief and zest for life, and
determine new aspirations for your future. These qualities were there
at your birth and they will underpin your quest to achieve your true
potential, for there is nothing you cannot accomplish with the power
of Love and Light. If you continue this exercise you will eventually
experience pearl and opalescent colours, the higher vibrations of
love energy, allowing you to transform and re-programme the divine
blueprint of your life.

Rachiel

Guardian Angel of Sexuality

I bring you the golden power of sexuality combined with true, unselfish love, for when reciprocated fully and completely between two persons it is riches indeed, and a way of bringing a piece of heaven to earth.

I guide you to use the powerful force of sexuality wisely and with deep love. How easy it is to fall in lust and to seek to gratify this urge! However, without love it is simply that: a gratification of the senses or animal passions. Without regard or respect for the other, what meaning does it have? But to infuse passion with true love is to bring sexuality to a different level, because then the desire is to please the other and not simply to please you.

I can be invoked, in the spirit of love and light, to assist you and your loved one with the prolonging of sexual pleasure, a desire that arises out of deep love. The powerful orgasmic energy released can be sent in a continuous golden loop from your heart over your head into the heart of your companion and then back to your heart. You can will and intend the energy to continue to travel in this loop for as long as possible, using the power of true love from your heart. You can also ask me to assist you to give healing to your loved one, through the power of love and sexual energy being generated. The more loving intent you give to this request, the more healing can be accomplished. Your partner can return healing to you also. Therefore, I remind you that if passion is to be meaningful it must be with the right partner and combined with true unselfish love; then the results of this for both can be powerful beyond imagining.

Rachmiel

Guardian Angel of Compassion

I descend to you on radiant rays of soft golden light, a light that is warm and full of compassionate love. Breathe it in to permeate your heart with comfort, easing anguish and bereavement, for I bring this gift to all those who need me.

I come to help all living creatures, but particularly those who cannot fend for themselves in this often-cruel world: the very young, the old, the sick and the animal kingdom. Once, my energy guided St Francis of Assisi to teach this lesson to mankind.

Especially I care for those who are sad, bereaved, tormented or lonely. Perhaps you need this infinite love and compassion at this very moment. While what is done may not be undone, it will ease with time. Though you may feel exhaustion within your soul so deep that you do not know how to begin to heal, with my assistance you will gradually find the means to let go of grief and despair in order to re-open your heart towards serenity and hope.

During a period of suffering I can be invoked from the heart, as I am often needed to bring gentle rays of healing to those frozen by grief or rejection, or immersed in bitter loneliness. Sit quietly and breathe in my loving, golden energy, allowing it to flow into your heart where its warmth will slowly start to dissolve your pain, releasing it from your body and mind with your tears, which are a form of deep cleansing. Let my golden ray reach towards your soul and comfort your spirit, for as that part of you, your wellspring of light, absorbs this energy it will gradually find a way to begin to radiate love once more. Do not feel afraid of opening to love again, for as you send it out to All Life it will be returned to you manifold.

Radueriel

Guardian Angel of Artistic Inspiration

I come to tell you that I, master of heavenly song, patron of artists, see that you have natural talent residing in your soul. It is filled with beauty that must be allowed expression, for it will assist others to find inspiration.

Whatever the medium you use, your creativity can give life to ideas and themes, which remain only vague and colourless to others. They have their own talents, to be sure, but your gifts are special, for you can communicate with clarity of vision and an innate sense of harmony. Among your skills is also subtlety, so that you see the interplay of colour, texture, light and sound, and can convey this variation. Where others might see only grey, you see the infinite shades within and can interpret their meanings. This might be in any form, for the medium itself does not matter, but conveying the message with all its nuances correctly is so very important. What you create is also a catharsis for you, allowing you to release pent-up issues, for your art is a tangible expression of the triumph of the human spirit.

You are guided by your wonderfully deep intuition, and I also come to assist, if invoked, with further developing this on behalf of your fellow man. Do not underestimate yourself, for you have the power to do great work; from your soul flows the intuitive knowledge of what truly matters in life. Because it transcends mere words, you communicate directly to the souls of others in a mystic synergy which cannot be learned but must be inborn. Use your talent, in whatever form you feel it is best expressed, for your inspirational work can achieve so much that would otherwise be lost.

Ramiel

Guardian Angel of Clarity

Mine is the silver light of Truth to clarify your vision. My wings are bright mirrors; look in them to see your reflection. I help you to recognize your true self, for you must love and respect yourself to appreciate your self-worth.

My light helps you to clarify purpose, motivation and vision. But first, when you look in my mirror do you see only your perceived shortcomings? Let go of judgement; when you start to appreciate yourself, you can objectively examine your talents, for they are many. Now consider those you love and try to view each of them with greater clarity. They, too, have their faults but nonetheless you love them. Do not, however, see only their strengths but refuse to recognise their many weaknesses, for they need your help to learn and grow from their lessons in life. Love them enough to know when to hold on and when to let go.

Now clarify what you would like to achieve in your life. Are your goals clear, or ghostlike through a fog of indecision? Let my silver light shine through and my love enlighten your thoughts, for the thicker this fog becomes the more you cannot see your real purpose in life and what will make you happy. When, together, we have dispelled this miasma, you must take the time to consider your situation carefully. View your goals reflected clearly in my mirrored wings, for when you have a vision, you are more than capable of seeing it through. With my infinite love to support your inner confidence, you will be motivated to start. Along with your new-found purpose, make your intention also clear and send as much positive energy as possible to this vision, trusting in the outcome until your dream is realized.

Rampel

Guardian Angel of Mountains

Through mighty upheaval of earth's heart are my mountains formed, towering into the clear blue sky and dazzling in their snowy purity. My sacred breath directs the glaciers and sends the deep waters to nestle in volcanic craters.

My stately energy directs the flow of the glaciers and I remind you that the slow, inexorable pace that they travel achieves as dramatic and powerful a result as a swift-flowing river. Be patient, like these glaciers, for this is the way that is more appropriate for you at this time. My mountains call to many, for the clean open spaces and breathtaking views allow mankind to breathe and visualize a world far removed from the daily grime and grind. You may be one who finds peace and tranquillity amid this beauty and, if so, do not neglect this call. It may be that your very soul is healed by communion with my mountains, for to gaze on such grandeur is a transcendental experience - a form of meditation.

Perhaps you find that your life and aspirations are reflected in the calm, still waters of my pools and this gives you new purpose and hope at a time of need. Whatever aspect of my guardianship you crave, I support you with my unconditional love until you are once more at peace with your inner self.

Raphael

Guardian of Sunday, the Sun and 2nd Heaven

I come on a pure golden spiral that flows from Father Sun to manifest all life on Mother Earth. It is the glorious energy ray whose nurturing warmth brings you joy of living, banishes darkness and enlightens your life and future.

My task is to guide you towards knowledge of self-healing, harmony and balance so that you can use this knowledge to help others. Consider your life as a canvas on which you can create any picture you like. To do this, however, you need health, else your picture will be faint indeed. You also require balance and harmony between the active, gold side of you and your passive, silver side. I aid the gold aspect of you: making decisions, using logic and analytical skills, and taking action accordingly; this is connected with the power of your will and mind. Your silver side - the power of your feelings and intuition - is ruled by the moon, whose guardian is Gabriel.

   If you would receive Love and Light through my golden rays, close your eyes and breathe in my energy. See the spiral of gold travel from the sun anti-clockwise down into your crown, then circle round your heart and flow into your solar plexus. Absorb as much gold as you can, for the solar plexus is where your will and mind power are located. To empower you further I can help you actually to ignite the sun within you, harnessing its healing power at many, even cellular, levels. I assist you then to send gold down through your energy centres to ground in earth, and up to your right brow third eye chakra where it will join and integrate with the silver energy of Gabriel. This will help you gradually to attain true harmony of mind and body and then you can move towards crown and spirit.

Raziel

Guardian Angel of the Celestial Secrets

I am charged with keeping the Book of Raziel, containing all the celestial secrets, for I am the embodiment of the secret wisdom of all races since the dawn of time and my book tells of the wondrous mysteries of paradise itself.

Mine was the hand that retrieved the book from safekeeping with the dolphins and whales, in order to give this wisdom to Adam to shape your world. Later I gave it to Noah to rebuild after the Flood; the book guided Moses and also Solomon the wise, who built the great Temple of Jerusalem with angelic assistance.

The secrets are not for all - they tell of the immensities of the heavens, weaving together science and mysticism. They contain astronomy, sacred geometry, the universal laws and their connections with the angelic hierarchy. If you are one who is drawn to my name, who seeks this knowledge for greater good, you can ask me to guide you. I will set in train the synchronicity to show you the path on which this knowledge can be learned and my wisdom revealed. My secrets have been handed down through the millennia, often hidden - the true meaning of the word 'occult' - but never lost. But I counsel you that the path to the celestial wisdom of my book can only be safely accessed by those chosen ones who work seriously, solemnly and selflessly for the benefit and in the service of all. When found they must be unlocked with integrity, absorbed with rightness and mastered with humility. If you are such a one your life will become enriched beyond measure, for my book reveals the true potentiality of mankind when lifted by the power and the understanding of All.

Rikbiel

Guardian Angel of the Power of Love

I drive the light chariot of the Creator, fashioned from dazzling golden rays, that travels at the speed of love to resolve and heal all problems, for whatever or wherever they are, be assured that love will find the way.

I help you to send the healing power of love. It may be that you have a personal situation to resolve, or you want to help a friend, or perhaps you wish to send healing to a war zone, to victims of an earthquake, or simply to the earth herself for healing damage inflicted by mankind.

How fast is the speed of love? It is faster than the speed of thought, and this is faster than the speed of light. One way to send love is through an in-breath and out-breath. Focus on the situation that you want to help, invoking me to guide your thoughts. Become a love centre for the purpose of healing or helping others. It may take a little time, so have patience, but every time you do this exercise there will be an effect, because you are sending unconditional love. Take a deep breath and imagine you are breathing in this power, the golden energy of pure love itself, the breath of the Father. Hold this golden breath, visualizing it as within your heart, and magnify it with the love in your heart as much as you possibly can. Then get ready and explode this breath out to heal the situation. As you breathe out this breath goes instantly to the problem, and love will gradually find a way to solve it. It also returns to you, the sender, at the speed of love, bringing back the golden energy, manifold, to heal you and your life, so the more you do this the more universal healing you will receive in return.

Rochel

Guardian Angel of Lost Things

I come to you in a bubble of golden energy - in this you may see if you will the things you have lost from your life. Look on and reflect, for some of these you perhaps wished to be rid of, but if others leave you bereft I am here to aid you.

Let us consider firstly what you may have lost from yourself. If you are unhappy about something within you, then think back to when you felt happy and fulfilled. Close your eyes and walk back in your mind to that time; see yourself surrounded by the people and places that contributed to this feeling. Evaluate what has happened since and what changed to bring about your sense of loss, and invoke my aid to retrieve this aspect of yourself in order to make yourself more complete, so long as it is for your ultimate benefit. Perhaps it is the child within that you lost somewhere down the years; I will help you to remember and bring back the simple joy that you once knew.

On the other hand, you may have physically lost something or someone very dear to your heart. If it is at all possible that it can be re-found, then I will come to your aid with my golden energy. Sit quietly and visualize the lost object or person in my bubble of gold, applying the power of your will to the vision. Invoke my name three times, asking with all your heart for it to be restored to you. Keep your faith and trust, and gradually things will start to happen. On many occasions you will find what was lost, but if you do not, it is because its part in your life is completed. Then both it and you must move on.

Ruhiel

Guardian Angel of the Winds

I am the voice of the winds of change, that blow away that which you wish to release from your life; I swirl in with my bright golden energy to allow new vigour to fill and surround you, so you are borne on my winds to new horizons.

Ponder on your life at present and invoke my assistance if you would harness my winds of change. If just a little change or healing is needed to boost your happiness, ask for the power of my gentle westerly wind to allow you to take a fresh, objective look at yourself and your situation. On the other hand, are you a person who makes the same mistakes over and over again, but does not know how to get rid of this programming? Invoke my help to bring the healing element of my north wind; by will and intent this contains the power to isolate and remove such programming from your mind. Write down what you want to remove, tear up the paper and let it and your old self go with my wind. Perhaps you are trapped in a murky situation, longing to break free? My east wind invigorates - invoke me to invite it in to blow away the fog from your mind, thus allowing clarity and opportunity for new pastures.

If you are not unhappy but feel set in your ways, and want to do something different that will stretch your intellect and bring new development and learning, I can send my warm and nurturing south wind to guide you. Visualize this wind of change bringing the possibility of expansion of your activities, new and fertile ideas and personal growth of a most beneficial kind, yet blowing you ever forward towards the Light.

Sachluph

Guardian Angel of Plants

My light shines through my lush green chains of foliage, the delicate tracery of ferns, in my flowers that master the deserts as well as gracing inhospitable mountainsides. It glows from the beauty of form that plants bring to mankind.

On the widest scale my plants protect Mother Earth in many ways. They preserve her soil, providing protection also for wildlife, as well as contributing to healing her atmosphere. When they die they fertilize and enrich the soil, and so the cycle continues. Before creatures walked this earth my plants grew to provide a beginning to all life.

Not only do I represent the actuality of living plants, but also the art forms within them. See the perfection of the petals of my flowers and the shape of my leaves, and witness how they soften and enhance your surroundings. As you gaze on green and absorb the colour, it helps to heal your heart of sadness through past relationship issues, and having done so, to promote new growth and expansion within yourself. That is why you instinctively like to look out upon the colour green. If it is not possible for you to do this, perhaps you can have one plant that you are nurturing in a pot. The health and growth of this plant will be pleasing to you, lifting your thoughts, and as the recipient of your care and attention, it is a symbol of your love for Mother Earth.

It is I who help you to cultivate plants and flowers of all hues and textures, so that their growth and flowering helps light up your life, so treat my plants tenderly as you would a dear friend. As you care for them, you are caring for me. Rest assured that everything you do is witnessed by angels.

Sahaqiel & Alphun

Guardian Angels of the Sky and Doves

Fly skyward with us on gilded wings, soaring into the celestial blue, like a golden dove seeking father sun. Gradually our secrets will be revealed, for the sky is the limit as your energy and enthusiasm set your spirit free.

We come to tell you that for you nothing is impossible, particularly for your spiritual aspirations, so we urge you to reach up to the stars! The sky and its inhabitants, including the clouds, the elements and rainbows, hold messages. Look up and see white birds flying, or a cloud shape of wing or feather, or a sudden rainbow appear, and know that this is for your spiritual guidance. On the path of your life, we send you three white feathers, and counsel you that there is much, much more than you can know in one lifetime.

Make the most of this opportunity we offer you, to guide this life path. It contains the promise of great spiritual development, and you may or may not have already embarked on this course. If you have not, then now is the time to make a start, and we will support you in this quest for appropriate direction. You need our golden rays of positive action to carry you forward. If you are already on this path, then rejoice! There is little you cannot accomplish if you really focus your energy, and once you have committed to the quest then we will ensure that synchronicity takes over. The more you accept and surrender, the more you will be shown, until your spirit reels with the wonder of life's secrets. Do not be daunted by the challenge of this real life quest. These are exciting times on planet earth - pledge yourself to reach for the sky and we will support you with our radiant wings of Love and Light.

Sandalphon

Guardian Angel of Prayer

I provide guidance on your spiritual quest - a shining path of light - gathering your prayers like flowers, whenever you think or speak them. Cushioned by cool and soft silver rays of love, I convey them to heaven on your behalf.

It does not matter whether you say your prayers formally, in a church, or informally when walking down the street or driving your car. I am always there when you need me, and I hear all your words, understanding your request and responding with tender care. If what you request be not for your highest good, then I comfort you and help you towards a different but more appropriate choice.

I urge you to listen for my guidance, allowing me to direct your footsteps from time to time, for the path of Light stretches ever ahead of you into the distance and you need to know how to reach it. Try to meditate, invoking me to be with you and to protect you - then listen with your heart. You may or may not hear my words, but still I am there, and will also show you signs from nature or through books and song to steer your way. I also come to you in dreams if you have been asking for my assistance. Sometimes I send three white feathers to signify I am with you, to help your spiritual development, for three is the number of Divine Truth. Or I may show my presence in the crimson or purple petals of a flower, for these are symbolic of my allotted heavenly task. For as I collect your prayers or invocations, I convert them to flowers of this hue and they ascend on my silver rays to the celestial city of the Creator.

Savatri

Guardian Angel of Sunlight

I bring you the power of the sun's rays even on the darkest day, for these rays manifest from my golden eyes to light up your existence. With these rays I illuminate your prayers and allow your heart and mind to be enlightened.

You may invoke me to aid you at any time, especially if your life seems particularly difficult and dark. Picture me directly above you, knowing that I protect you with my love. Breathe deeply, imagining that you can draw in the rays emanating from my eyes down into your crown chakra to fill your head with golden light. Let this energy banish gloomy, negative or depressive thoughts, for they cannot survive the presence of my radiance. As my light floods your mind, let your depression lift and evaporate like mist before sunlight. Now allow the golden light to fill your heart, expanding it with love, and then use the power of your intent to see it flow and cascade throughout your body. This light will bring you divine angelic comfort and healing.

Finally, let my golden ray flow and shine within your skin and pores, so that you are filled with radiant light. Even in winter the strength of your will can make this happen. Then will and intend it to flow to your aura, where it will surround you like a swirling golden ball of invisible light. With your own willpower and at any time, visualize this golden energy around you, emanating from your heart. Whatever the weather outside, you can send this golden healing, the blessing of the sun, giver of life, to those around you who are in need. Or you could will it to go to world catastrophes or conflicts, knowing that some of its healing will reach others through the power of love itself.

Seraphiel

Guardian Angel of Cosmic Spirit Quintessence

In a column of diamond brilliance I descend, my eyes are the stars and constellations are formed from the splendour of my wings; I am the music of the spheres and the light of Source from the Creator made manifest.

When I am with you it is as if the air around you were visible in a million rainbow molecules, as though it were newly created, which in a sense it is. My celestial music resonates within your soul and empowers your spirit. In your duality world Source becomes golden star fire above, and silver earth flame below, but through me it is re-united and made whole once again, into crystalline diamond strands of existence where all colours and shades of creation are in perfect harmony. Ponder this in your heart - are you one who strives towards Unity for mankind and works for the cause of the Light?

If so, with your loving will and intention you can draw down my quintessential ray of cosmic spirit. Breathe it in through your crown with a sacred in-breath, making your body a column filled with diamond light energy. Magnify the energy with the power of your spirit and then breathe it out on a sacred out-breath to All Life. From there, at the speed of love, you will receive it back manifold, the diamond rays infusing and healing spirit and then mind and body at all levels. With my help, the flower of your heart centre will integrate and become a geometric crystal that will then connect through sacred geometry to All Life, bringing universal harmony and aiding your light work further. Ground and manifest as much of my energy as you can, for this is the task your spirit chose to do aeons ago at the proper time, and that time is now.

Shekinah

Twin Guardian of the Tree of Life

My white-gold radiance is brighter than the sun itself as it flows to surround and nurture the Tree of Life. I guard the tree as it grows in the earthly kingdom, its roots and crown a glorious symbol of your spiritual quest.

I am twin to Metatron, who is guardian of the crown of the tree; while Metatron aids your spirituality, I guide your earthly life and love. I may be invoked to bless your choice of life partner, for if your foundations in this life are happy and secure you will be able to build upon these to climb on your spiritual journey to crown. If you are lonely, or filled with sorrow or hurt, your soul will be constricted and less able to expand in spiritual development; you will not progress far from the foot of the tree.

Let go of low self-esteem or feelings that you do not deserve to be happy - of course you deserve love and joyful partnership in your life. You may invoke me at any time, affirming your need often and positively, and trusting in the outcome. My radiance helps to heal all wounds caused by love, allowing you to transcend unhappiness and past hurts in order to find a new and fulfilling relationship. As I am a mirror image and reflection of Metatron, earthly love, when true and unselfish, is but a reflection of the love of the Creator. When your love is given to the right partner it heals and strengthens, bringing in return confidence and energy and helping your spiritual quest, for this makes and gradually deepens your divine connection. The Tree of Life symbol is in reverse - its roots are above and its crown below, for in the eternal cycle, its seed, or end, is once again its beginning, or new life.

Sofiel

Guardian Angel of Earth's Bounty

I spring on golden rays from Mother Earth, with all her richness, beauty and magnificence, and her nurturing fruitfulness. I bring my golden philosophy containing a threefold message of Truth for you on wholeness and wellbeing.

Firstly, eat correctly. This means eating wisely with real food, for this is the food that will help you to be healthy. Turn away from additives, substitutes and chemicals that may be harming you on a long-term basis. Choose your raw materials with care and cook them yourself so that you know and trust what you are eating. Remember that food is energy that powers your bodily strength, and if you do not eat wisely you are depleting your energy levels and therefore your own zest for life. Drink enough water, for your body is mostly composed of water and needs a sufficient daily intake to maintain its organs. Invoke me to assist you with moderation in your appetite, for this is important.

Secondly, breathe properly. Wherever and whenever you can, breathe clean air, as deeply as possible, drawing it down into your lungs. Many people take shallow breaths, and this seriously affects the functioning of the energy centres of the body. To breathe correctly is to help the body to be well. Try to give up any damaging habits and focus on a more wholesome attitude to your body.

Thirdly, I ask you to respect Mother Earth. Do whatever you can to help heal her. This may not be much, but every little helps. Think how Mother Earth and her elements maintain your life, how her fruits give you health and, as you gaze upon her beauty, pledge to give her as much love as you can in return.

Spugliguel

Guardian Angel of Spring

I am the golden glow that causes the trees to open their new leaves in a bright canopy of green, and the foliage to deliver its glory once again, for mine is a season of great beauty and promise that you, too, can harness.

I rule the vigorous time of the year when nature brings expansion, fresh growth and vivid colour. Put the past behind you and make plans for your own new spring, for I bring you the same opportunity to make a fresh start in your own life. But in the same way that nature chooses the strongest seeds from which to send forth her buds and then her shoots, so must you first determine the best options for your new start. Remember that during my springtime all the roots for new growth will be made, so that sufficient strength is assured to set the scene for summer's plenty. Ensure that you, too, have a firm foundation upon which to build. The sunshine and rain of my season bring potentially rapid development, but translated into the framework of a joyful life you also need this expansion to be controlled and managed.

Use winter, the time of rest and recuperation, to take stock of your current position and to consider what it is you really wish to achieve. Take this time to evaluate your personal strengths, upon which you can build, while working with my aid to overcome your weaknesses. Then make the plans that need to be made in good time to bring about your own spring resurgence. As the season turns I bring loving support as you sow your own seeds for a future filled with abundance. I nurture them with my golden light energy so that they grow strong and beautiful to help you achieve your true and full potential.

Tabris

Guardian Angel of Free Will

I beckon to you from the Door to Light, out of which the golden radiance of my splendour shines forth. I seek to guide your footsteps and choices, for many are the doors that open during your life, but few will be your Doors to Light.

Heed my call if you would change your life to become more at peace with yourself. It may be that your eye does not yet see the light that pours from this door. You may be concerned with material or day-to-day issues in your life, which blind you to your true purpose - finding happiness and fulfilment. What is the point of filling your home with riches if you have no time or peace to enjoy them? If your life feels unfulfilled it may be because you are viewing your goals only with the eye and not with the heart. The Creator gave you choice in all things. You can choose to receive my dazzling golden radiance into your heart, the light that will show you the spiritual way forward to find your golden path of true wholeness.

   If you have already walked through your first Door to Light, and still wish to invoke my aid, then I help you to negotiate the way to your next door. For always there are choices to make, crossroads to negotiate, different doors presented. I see your higher purpose and the needs of your spirit as well as your mind and body. I am the golden power of your higher self; you may invoke my loving support whenever you wish to guide the decisions that you make, to help you to choose the Way of Love and Light.

Tagas

Guardian Angel of Music

I sound the silver chord that comes from the void to resonate with your soul in the melodies of life. My silver wings trail music from the stars to teach you the power of musical harmony, and enrich your world with joyful angelic song.

I remind you that with song you come closer to the angels on the vibration of harmonic sound. Let your soul be lifted skywards like the lark as it flies towards the sun, borne aloft as it seems by the sheer silvery power of its liquid notes. For music is another means of healing. Bring melody into your life in any way that seems right. If you play an instrument, play it with sheer joy. If not, sing aloud to raise your spirits and brighten your day, or to lift sadness or depression, for with me you have the voice of an angel.

Now imagine your whole being as a musical chord. Your body is made up of seven major energy centres (chakras), each of which has a colour and a sound vibration, in fact a musical note. If all is balanced, then the notes together will make up a harmonious and beautiful chord. On the other hand, if they are not balanced or if one or more are blocked, then you have discord.

Think of how your very soul expands with harmony or contracts with disharmony. Work to make your body more melodic by listening with your heart to your favourite musical sound vibration and letting the notes resonate through your soul. All things on Mother Earth - and indeed in the universe itself - contain certain vibrations of sound and light. As you harmonize yourself, then you also place yourself in harmony with the wondrous symphony that is all of creation.

Thuriel & Anpiel

Guardian Angels of Wild Birds and Animals

Ours are the wild creatures whose grace and strength enhance the beauty of Mother Earth. Your care and love for these creatures develop your link to the collective consciousness that unifies All Life as made by the Creator.

If you are an admirer of wild animals and birds, caring for those who come near to your home, then we send you our shimmering silver energy in thanks for your unselfishness. The wild creatures that come to your garden are part of life's pattern, and giving a little food in winter shows your love. Through actions such as these you are pursuing your personal spiritual path.

Though you cannot care for some of our creatures of mountains or deserts, you admire them from afar and they serve to inspire your thoughts and dreams. The denizens of lakes, forests and jungles aid the ecological balance; send them loving energy as they fight for survival. As they must battle with the elements and man's depredations, you too must sometimes fight battles in life. If this resonates with you, invoke our guidance and look for our responses through wild animals and birds or pictures of them. For example, the swan exemplifies a need for faithfulness and loyalty, the robin or eagle means we are near and are guiding your spiritual path. Through a white dove or three white feathers we send you a message of peace and spirituality. A snake tells you to seek wisdom or, by the shedding of his skin, offers chance of transformation. A deer signifies a need for gentleness, a bull is a sign to be patient, an elephant means strength as well as wisdom, a tiger is for financial luck and a horse symbolizes dependability for others.

Torquaret

Guardian Angel of Autumn

In a silver drift of frost-rimed leaves I come, swirling and eddying in the autumn wind that can blow away your past. In my season there is great beauty of colour and form, but it is also a time for your personal reckoning.

Autumn is the time to review the result of the promise of spring and whether this promise was delivered in summer. It is the time for reaping, and afterwards for retrenchment and preparation for the quiet time of winter. It is the same in your life. What you planted in your spring, if correctly nurtured, came to fruition in your summer. Think back: how happy were you with your summer abundance? Did you plant wisely and nurture faithfully? Remember, it is your harvest that you reap and you are the harvester.

   If you reaped abundant joy, then I underpin that joy with my love, so that you can build upon it to bring about an even greater harvest next year. If not, I guide you now to take stock of your present life, for this is your chance to determine a different future. It is an opportunity for you to cleanse the past, sweeping it away like my autumn drifts of leaves. I bring my silver feminine energy to help you use your intuitive skills, thinking with both heart and head. Prune out that which you wish to be rid of from your life, making a bonfire to burn old behavioural patterns. In short, ensure that all is well and the earth of your life is cleared. Then it can be rested and recharged during winter's quiet dormant time. Have the courage and determination to be ready for replanting in the new spring, for though my gentle silver wings support your efforts, all your future potential lies finally in your own two hands.

Tual

Guardian Angel of Taurus and April

I come to you on gilded wings of light, filled with the strength and patience of my bull sign. As my season of the year heralds awakening and new life, I bring you positive golden energy to start reviewing and simplifying your life.

I praise your dependability in delivering the things that you undertake. Even at personal cost, if you have given your word to something or someone, you will not let them down. Generally you think things through systematically, but you are reluctant to take too many chances or risks - you like to deal only in certainties! Unfortunately, life is not always certain; invoke me to guide you in whether to go forward or draw back.

You have worked hard to achieve your aims, and are surrounded by the success you deserve. But there comes a time when you must decide that the mental or physical things you cling to are in fact complicating your life. The people whose burdens you have accepted must eventually be allowed to be independent. You must also learn to say no to a situation, for though others view you as a stabilizing force in their world, your own life becomes out of balance by taking on too many responsibilities. Also, you prevent those who should be shouldering their own burdens from learning by their experiences. I counsel you to begin de-cluttering your life. My calming golden rays flow to surround you now so that you can clarify and review your situation, deciding where to hold on and when to let go, for as you simplify your issues you will create a calmer, less complicated and more focused future.

Tubiel

Guardian Angel of Summer and Tame Birds

In yellow rays of golden sun you will find me, for my season is one of life-giving light. Close your eyes and smell the flower scents that enhance my days, and harvest this time of blossom and plenty for yourself and your life.

Mine, too, are the birds that you may keep as pets for their beauty and song, or who frequent your garden every day. They can inspire by example. My birds can also comfort and guide you or lighten your days; their colours, antics and friendly activities can heal and renew. By loving and caring for my bright creatures you express your love for me as well as for nature herself.

Visualize my glorious season as a metaphor for the enrichment of your own life and make the most of this burgeoning by capitalizing on your many life opportunities. As golden summer is the time of my fruition, so you can also complete projects and so make reality of your dreams and ambitions. However you should ensure that before my season you have made all the necessary plans. Use colour to assist. First, with the power of red, secure and re-affirm the foundations of your life, empowering yourself with energy and determination, so that you can plant the seeds of your new future in appropriate and well-prepared soil. With orange, allow your creativity free rein, for this is the time to innovate and transform life. Then, as my golden season unfolds, your carefully planted and nurtured life seeds will ripen and reach their summer magnificence. This is the time to absorb yellow, to fully activate your willpower to succeed, and I urge you to take this opportunity I offer you to achieve new heights of personal development.

Umabiel

Guardian Angel of Astrology

My wings hold the brilliance and purity of stars and my silver radiance illumines their meaning for mankind. All knowledge is written in my heavenly bodies and I reflect this celestial radiance down to enlighten your very soul.

The secrets of your own heavenly blueprint are written in my stars, there for you to discover and unravel. Have you ever gazed at my stars in the velvet night sky, wondering what message they hold? To find what was ordained when your soul incarnated, study your birth chart. Invoke my name to aid you and take steps to find a skilled person to construct and read the chart for you, so that you can learn and absorb its message. Through your astrological path there are still points at which you will have choices to make; my loving support will guide you to choose the doors leading to light and spirituality.

It may also be that you could be gifted in reading and interpreting information from the stars. For millennia man has studied my mysteries. Indeed, you may have done this before in a past life and so you are often drawn to the wisdom unfolding from my stars. You do not need special skills, for all can be learnt, and much is down to intuition. If you are drawn to unravelling this wisdom, and if my constellations hold a fascination for you, then study this ancient discipline. It may take a little time - though what is time in astrological terms? As you grow in confidence you will find the answers to your own questions, and be able to help others. Many will come to you then for interpretation, for you will guide them on the influence of stars in their future hopes and dreams.

Uriel

Guardian Angel of Fire and Alchemy

*Many and mysterious are the ways I manifest on Mother Earth.
I can descend in dazzling lightning, bringing you my magical
cleansing and purifying fire of alchemy, and then offer the power
of creativity, innovation and transformation.*

Have you ever sat by a fireside, gazing into the flames, and wondering
what magic they hold? I offer you the chance to journey in your
imagination into these flames - let the tongues of fire reach out
towards you with their colours of power. Visualize your mind, body
and spirit dissolving and becoming one with the flames. First they
gently surge within the energy meridians of your body, for they are
the fire of cleansing and purification. All old programming can be
burnt away and all blocks within your chakra system rendered down
to ash; even this may be scoured clean by my magic fire.

Now, replenish with the colours of fire. Breathe in the power
of the sun's fire to your solar plexus area, the location of your
willpower. This yellow flame can ignite the sun itself within your
body ,after which all is achievable with power of will and mind, and
with loving intent. Next, the focus moves to amber (the fire of a
thousand suns). Breathe this energy to kindle the orange flame of
your own creative force within you, your promise of innovation and
self-transformation. Move down to root chakra, and breathe in red
fire. This energizes and empowers you, securing the foundation on
which to build your new self. Collectively, my alchemy flames bring
infinite possibility - will you take advantage of my aid, and like my
mystical phoenix, soar reborn and more beautiful from my
alchemical flames to find glorious new beginnings?

Vasariah

Guardian Angel of Finances

Mine is the shining ray that brings financial astuteness, an enabling energy to repair and reinforce your chalice of life, for if you do not face and tackle your money issues the beautiful gold of joy and abundance will be dissipated.

If financial worries are clouding your judgement or consuming your waking thoughts, and preventing you from seeing your way forward, I come to aid you. But if your worries concern another - perhaps a child, or friend - you must send them love but let them go. You cannot protect others from their mistakes. They need them, for how otherwise do they learn the rules of the game of life? Life is given to each individual to make their own progress, and though you can, if asked, advise others, you cannot live life for them.

Focus on your own finances and imagine your life as a chalice, potentially full to the brim with the liquid gold of joy and abundance. Now see your chalice contains cracks, formed from your worries and past money mistakes, issues whose ramifications are with you still. See how the potential leaks out and is wasted, so your chalice is never full! First you must take ownership of your personal situation, and assume responsibility for repairing the cracks, so that your cup can be replenished. Invoke my assistance to bring loving support, as you start to review your finances. My energy aids you with positive steps to evaluate your situation, and make plans where necessary gradually to put your affairs in order. As you do so, little by little your worries will diminish and one by one the cracks in your chalice of life will be repaired. In due course, as your financial situation is resolved, the last crack will disappear; your chalice will not only fill but will overflow with the pure gold of peace of mind.

Verchiel

Guardian Angel of July and Leo

With the glorious strength and steadfast courage of the lion of my sign, I come on my tawny wings to aid you, for my loving energy brings you the confident leadership ability to inspire the hearts of others with your power of vision.

Though you, yourself, sometimes need reassurance, you are one who has the ability to fire the passions and enthusiasm in those around you, engendering the loyalty needed to follow your lead and accept your guidance, for they will understand that what you plan is for their own ultimate benefit. You have the power of vision and a caring energy that carries others into a cause. Once this golden fire is ignited within you, then so much will be achievable, for you will inspire a group whose energy, ignited in turn, will be far greater than the sum of the individuals might suggest. Just such a situation is arising or will arise, and even now you may be wondering if you really do have the skills needed to take on this responsibility and lead it to a satisfactory conclusion. Let go of any self-doubt - I urge you to accept and believe that you do indeed have the potential to do this, for you are supported by the golden power of my love. No matter if in some ways you are untested, this is your opportunity to put your innate skills to excellent use.

If you so choose, I will be with you as you grow and learn with this experience, increasing your self-confidence. Those who follow you will also develop, and through it all the consequence will be that your future - and theirs - will be reshaped in new and exciting ways.

Yusamin

Guardian Angel of Fertility

From the wellsprings of Love and Light I stream, on shining wings fashioned from living light itself. I carry in my heart the silver seeds of fertility and the power of love to make all things grow and flourish for the highest good.

Perhaps it is for the fertility of your body that you seek my help. To aid conception you can invoke me to assist, when the time is right, and if it is for the benefit of all concerned; if not, I guide you to wait a little longer.

   I also aid you with fertility of mind - new ideas and concepts - for you may have found that your job or relationship has lately become dull and stale. Life should never be thus - it is your perception that makes it seem so and it may be time to make changes. Let the purity of my silver light first fill and illuminate your mind, chasing away the shadows that clouded your thoughts and freeing your throat, so that you can speak your truth. This will enable you to see more clearly what you should do. When you come to speak, your very words will be imbued with the silver ray of calmness and clarity.

   When my light shines upon you, it can be absorbed into every fibre, so that you feel completely bathed and cleansed in its glory. Remember that whether you seek my aid for mind, body or spirit the cleansing is necessary before new growth can take place. Then renewed fertility of your mind and energizing of your body will generate opportunities which you had not thought possible, and soon your ideas will flourish, bringing excitement and enrichment to your future. New fertility of spirit will take you on adventures to learn the mystery of life along the silver spiral of wisdom itself that flows, like myself, from the living wellsprings of Love and Light.

Zadkiel

Guardian of Thursday, Jupiter and 6th Heaven

Mine is the golden light of wisdom that flows in an infinite spiral of divine proportion through all creation. With no beginning and no end, carrying within it abundance of all knowledge and opportunity, it circles around your heart.

Invoke me whenever you wish my golden rays of warm and loving energy to support your life and your surroundings. Abundance of all kinds can flow to you with my assistance, including opportunity, intelligence and generosity. If asked, I guide your prospects for success, knowing that you will share your abundance with others, for in this very sharing you will benefit as much as they from this synergy of Love and Lght.

   I come to reassure you that there is a great deal in your personality that people admire, not least your integrity, steadfastness and willingness to share your blessings. Your strength of character, idealism and refusal to compromise your principles has set standards that others envy. But things are not always as straightforward as you would wish, and you may be wondering if your moral view of right and wrong is mistaken. Your vision is not flawed, but your beliefs will be tested - let them withstand these tests and emerge stronger, yet refined like gold tempered in a fire, for this testing is part of your path. Will you compromise or retain your great integrity? If you pass this test, I bring you the power of gold to help you to retrieve your own ancient wisdom, for you have the means of great potential achievement in your life. You have forgotten much that once you knew, but with my loving support you will fly with me to the first point on my eternal golden spiral of wisdom. This is for abundance of remembering - wisdom has no beginning and no end, in its end is its beginning.

Zephon

Guardian Angel of Vigilance

I am the angel whose myriad golden eyes are ever alert to care for you and whose vigilance is unceasing and eternal. My golden energy is your secret armour as my love enfolds, protects and watches over your progress.

Many are the choices and challenges you will face, but if threatened or worried you may call my name for loving support, for though you may miss much my golden eyes of watchfulness see all.

Perhaps you are even now speeding into a situation, without fully thinking through the true implications of your action upon yourself and others around you. Invoke me to guide your awareness of the consequences of this action, and to help you to think things through a little more fully before it is too late. Though there are lessons you need to learn, not least to take more time and consideration where appropriate, still I may be called upon to guide your steps in this instance. Mankind has a saying that to be forewarned is to be forearmed. Invoke my aid for your forewarning, so that my golden love becomes your armour, and together we will go forward to meet this challenge.

I urge you also to pursue the path of integrity, honesty and respect for others, and to be vigilant in all your dealings, for there are many who will not treat you in the same way. Avoid those who lack these virtues, because if you give them your trust they are likely to let you down. Therefore, as you travel your road, I send you golden energy to support your quest, enabling you to be careful and watchful while ever travelling along the path of your life.

Zeruch

Guardian Angel of Strength

I am the arm of God. On wings that are stronger than a thousand eagles I descend to sustain you. Invoke me from your heart to uphold you in these wings, allowing my warm golden strength to flow into you and fill your body.

Many is the time when you will need my help - perhaps at this very moment you should call on me for my loving support, for nothing in your reality has a greater strength than I. There will be issues in your life during which you feel you are sinking under pressures - be they physical, mental or emotional - and bereft of the power to pull yourself free. Though it is not possible to live a life without any such traumas, my strength can be with you, for you have always known my name, but perhaps, at this moment, not in your conscious mind.

Where you may need my help most is for the strength you must find to deal with issues in your past or present. While you feel trapped, you cannot move forward correctly and achieve your potential. If this is the case, take the time first to reflect calmly in your heart of hearts on what you know you must do. I aid you with the mental and emotional courage that may be needed. Next, make a plan; invoke me to give you the strong willpower and tenacity to do what you have determined upon. Then use my assistance to take action. My love can help you take firm action to clear difficult entanglements detrimental to you. You can then reshape your present, for you will be free to live your life in a more positive way, establishing yourself in strength for all eternity.

Zikiel

Guardian Angel of Comets and Meteors

I descend in a silver cloud of cosmic dust, emanating like my comets from the outer limits of your Universe to tell of man's galactic origins. Like my denizens from deep space I flash past Mother Earth, trailing my silver mysteries.

You may invoke me, as I pass, to bring you the sudden brilliant flash of inspiration that you might need to make a quantum leap in life. If such inspiration is what you desire, place my name where you can see it, and invoke me to aid you, until you receive your insight.

My meteorites often appear as shooting stars (that you may wish upon), or they may land on earth, carrying other world influence directly to this planet. In them is found the extra-terrestrial crystal moldavite tektite, bringing its own special secrets to be unravelled by mankind. If you feel drawn to my meteorites, moldavite crystals and galactic wisdom, you may need to seek out one of these crystals to own. It need not be large, but when you find a selection, hold each in your hand and decide which seems to communicate with you. Use your intuition and your heart rather than your brain, for by this means the right crystal will be obvious to you immediately. You will feel or sense something special from this crystal.

When you have acquired your crystal you need do little more than keep it nearby or on your person, allowing it to convey its insights to you as and when the time is right. This will be the start of some life-changing experiences for you that will help you to understand your own origin, the reason why you are here on Mother Earth, and your specific role and higher purpose at this time.

Zuphlas

Guardian Angel of Trees

In silver zephyrs of wind I guide to Mother Earth, where my wings tenderly rustle and caress my trees. Newborn, slender or mighty, all are mine, and when you care for one of my trees, giving it your love, you embrace me also.

My trees help to stabilise Mother Earth, as well as producing oxygen, breath of life for mankind. They also hold much ancient wisdom; through communing with trees, by walking in woods or sitting beneath an ancient oak, you can receive a little of this wisdom. You may carve my wood if you are using it with love, but do not cut my trees down frivolously, for if you do so you cut at the heart of Mother Earth. Consider the loveliness of my trees in all four seasons, and their use as homes by wildlife. Cut down the sustainable forests with care and love, but please, never merely with greed.

Use an allegory of my trees in your own life. Plant your roots with care, in fertile ground, and nourish yourself correctly. Draw in the elements and their angels: good earth for firm roots, clean air to give life, sunshine and clear, unpolluted water to grow tall and true. Without these elements, like my trees, you will be stunted and weak, so if you would be sturdy and strong, think carefully on my words. Let the example of my trees teach you to live each stage of your life more carefully and wisely.

When you feel stressed, try to walk in my calm woodlands or among the grandeur of my forests for comfort and relaxation. Enjoy the quiet and tranquillity and absorb the healing peace into your very soul.

Zuriel

Guardian Angel of Libra and September

Mine is the pure golden energy that fills the scales of your life to the brim with love, to help balance and guide your decisions, and when these decisions are life transforming I give you my golden eyes to perceive your higher purpose.

As my star sign suggests, I support your straightforwardness, balance and conformity, for these are qualities of inner strength. However, I counsel you that this very strength can sometimes constrain you when you may need to break out of your old behavioural patterns in life to allow the new you emerge. Do not be afraid to change, for all life is a journey of experience towards maturity.

You have a decision pending at present, and I urge you not to prevaricate in this instance. I remind you that you could lose out on an important new opportunity by waiting too long to make up your mind, because of your second or third thoughts about making life transforming changes. Invoke me to fill your eyes with my loving golden energy, so that light helps you to see the scales more clearly. On one scale place the pros and cons of this decision, as it will concern either work or home, involving relationships to your work or even where you will live. On the other scale place your current life, whether or not you are happy as you are, and if deep down you want to make changes. Because this is a decision of much future consequence, now add love to the balance, and then view the result with your intellect as well as your eyes and your heart. If you invoke my guidance and ask for your decision to be for your highest good, I will guide your choice in the name of Love and Light.

GROUNDING AND BALANCING WITH THE CADUCEUS

The caduceus is an ancient symbol of grounding, balance and healing. The rod itself signifies wisdom of earth (grounding of the physical self) joining with wisdom of air (third eye spiritual connection), and also represents the human spine. Though usually shown in the hand of Raphael (patron angel of healing and the sun), the two (gold and silver) snakes of wisdom represent balance of both solar (Raphael) and lunar (Gabriel) energy. The points where the snakes cross the rod (or spine) represent the chakra energy centres of your body from base to third eye, and aid balance to that point. (Metatron and Shekinah, the twin angels of the Tree of Life, guide your balance below root and at crown). To use the caduceus daily for grounding, healing and balancing, make a pyramid shape above your head with your arms, joining your two palms, pointing upwards.

🐦 Invoke both Raphael and Gabriel, asking them to place the caduceus from All There is Above right through your spine, down into the heart of All There is Below, from Father Sun to the very heart of Mother Earth.

🐦 Ask for energies of sun and moon, silver and gold, star fire and sacred flame to be cleansed through the power of your mind, body and spirit.

🐦 Then visualize the two rays winding back up your spine.

🐦 Ask the angels for healing and polarity balance as the snakes cross each chakra centre (they will cross six times).

🐦 As they cross, starting from base, you can say: *"left and right"*, *"masculine and feminine"*, *"sun and moon"*, *"silver and gold"*, *"star fire and sacred flame"*, *"Raphael and Gabriel"*.

🐦 At this point they link together, within the two angel wings at your third eye chakra, which completes this exercise. Remember to thank Raphael and Gabriel, sending them your Love and Light in return for their help.

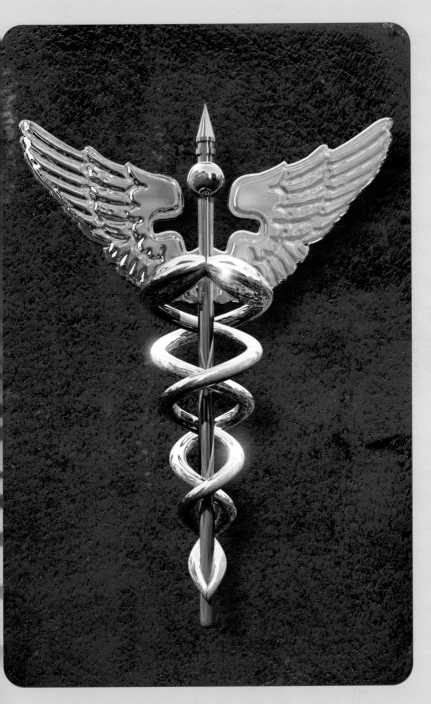

BREATHING IN GOLD OR SILVER

If you don't have time (or prefer not) to do a meditation, you can simply sit quietly (indoors or outdoors), take a deep in-breath and, as you invoke the angel that you wish to help you, imagine silver or gold pouring into the crown of your head. Remember that gold will generally energize you, and silver will be more relaxing. Bring in both if you feel you need balance. From there, visualize it streaming down until it reaches your heart, filling it with your chosen energy. Visualize it radiating from your heart throughout your body, making it glow at all levels. Then imagine breathing out the silver or gold to brighten the aura that surrounds you. If you do this exercise for a few minutes you will not only fill yourself with this beautiful healing energy, but also create an invisible but radiant sphere around you; you can ask the angels to help maintain it.

A SIMPLE GOLD OR SILVER MEDITATION

If you have a little more time (say 20-30 minutes), you could do a short angel meditation. Here is a simple meditation you can use to bring in the silver or gold energy of the guardian angel you have chosen to help you. Try this to really feel the Love and Light contained in your message from the angels. By quietly sitting to do this meditation, focusing your attention on your angel, you will also be in a position to receive further guidance, for how can the angels guide you if you don't give them the opportunity? Try to ensure that you will not be disturbed. Find a quiet place, or put on some relaxing music, and make sure you are comfortable before you start:

🪶 Take some slow, deep breaths in and out and try to focus on your inner self. As you breathe inwards, if you wish, you can say the words "*I breathe in pure positive energy*" (one of the descriptions of angels), and as your breathe outwards you could say "*I breathe out all negative emotions*".

- Feel yourself relaxing and going deeper into your inner self. Let external sounds become part of the background, and maintain your focus within.

- Imagine a column or meridian line within your body, extending in a vertical line downwards (it actually goes through the chakra points). It runs from the crown of your head right down your spine (the core of your being) and finishes at the base of the spine, which is the root of your being.

- Now visualize your angel's gold or silver light pouring into your crown, and feel this wonderful energy flowing down the meridian line and completely filling the column within your body.

- When the meridian is filled, the gold or silver rays will radiate outwards into the rest of your body.

- Send the energy to empower your will, and to fill your soul and your spirit.

- Ground, by sending the energy down your legs through your feet and right to the heart of Mother Earth.

- Invoke your angel three times by name, asking for special guidance or clarification of any gold or silver message you received.

- Now try to place your consciousness in your heart rather than your head, to see what you feel in response.

- A feeling of comfort and energy (warm for gold or cool for silver) will become apparent. If you trust in the angels, you will receive guidance and support. This could be in the form of words in your head, a sense of lightness or colours in your inner vision. Also, your request will set in motion a certain synchronicity of events that begin after this invocation, and gradually start to enlighten you.

Finally, thank your angels and send Love and Light in return, from your heart.

COLOUR AND THE CHAKRA ENERGY CENTRES

The chakras (Sanskrit for 'wheel') of the body are the energy centres that power your physical, mental and emotional health and vitality. The seven main chakras vibrate in the seven rainbow colours (plus magenta, the colour between violet and red, for the higher heart). The colours vibrate at different speeds, starting from the densest, red at base chakra, to the highest, violet at crown chakra, and above this pure white, Unity of all colours.

Apart from the colours, each is associated with angels and special symbols. On the chart opposite you will see the angels linked to each chakra from root to crown. There are also links with the planets of the solar system and with musical notes, as all is part of the harmonic of Creation, and the mystic significance of Sacred Seven. Above the crown is your connection to cosmic spirit, or Source, (also known as the Quintessence, fifth element), with music of the spheres and the angel Seraphiel. All vibrations need to be attuned correctly to achieve full wellbeing.

As you work through the colours, healing yourself and your life, you gradually attain balance and integration between aspects of self, and harmonize yourself physically and spiritually. As your consciousness expands, the colours gradually become paler and more refined. Eventually you receive pastels, pearly or opalescent shades; these are the highest vibrations that we can work with at present. Similarly, it seems that the musical notes of your chakras also become refined as you work towards greater spirituality, divine connection and universal harmony.

CHAKRA	ANGEL(S)		NOTE	UNIVERSAL CONNECTION
Crown	Metatron		B	Tree of Life - crown and spirit
Third Eye	Ariel and Melchisadec		A	Pluto
Throat	Michael and Zadkiel		G	Mercury and Jupiter
Heart	Haniel Phuel and Gabriel		F	Venus Moon and Neptune
Solar	Raphael		E	Sun (and all galactic suns)
Sacral	Uriel		D	Uranus
Base	Camael and Cassiel		C	Saturn and Mars
Below Base	Shekinah		C	Tree of Life - Mother Earth

CHAKRA AFFIRMATIONS WITH THE ANGELS

One way of starting to bring change on a particular life issue is to do a daily affirmation with the angel, a colour and a chakra energy centre. This will help you to focus as much positive energy and intent on your goal as you can. You can devise your own affirmation (in which case, keep it short for greater focus) or choose one from those shown below. Write the words on a card and place it somewhere you will see it every day. You could also do a brief meditation, making your affirmation at the same time, until you feel things are changing. The more positive intent you put into your affirmation, the more effective it will be. For relevant angels to invoke, refer to the chakra chart on page 127.

🍃 Root chakra and red build secure foundations for a better future.
"As I energize, secure and reaffirm my earthly life, I am empowered."

🍃 Sacral chakra and orange/amber (fire of a thousand suns) bring change.
"As the fire of creativity burns within, I innovate and transform."

🍃 Solar chakra and yellow helps you to succeed in your goals.
"With will and mind I ignite the power of the sun within me."

🍃 Heart chakras (and thymus). Firstly, emerald green or blue-green healing of water of love and life soothes and heals personal heart issues, then magenta allows the heart to open like a flower to unconditional love.
"As water of life heals my heart, it flowers with unconditional love and compassion."

🍃 Throat chakra and blue lead you to personal and absolute Truth.
"With the sword of truth I embrace abundance, wisdom and freedom."

🍃 Third eye chakra and purple are your psychic and spiritual link to other realities.

"With the power of earth, air and Spirit, I pierce the veil and transmute all illusion."

🍃 Crown chakra and pure white are your spiritual link to the Divine and heavenly peace.

"Through crown I deepen my divine connection and seek universal harmony."

🍃 Above crown is your link to Cosmic Spirit (also known as Source or Quintessence)

"I pledge myself to the cause of light and channel cosmic spirit for the benefit of all life."

BUILDING UP THE ENERGY

There are many ways of adding extra energy to your angelic invocations, affirmations or meditations. For example, by holding a crystal of an associated colour you add the power of that crystal. Refer to the page on the angel Och in the A-Z for information on the crystals linked to the chakra centres. You can also use a flower or gem essence on your pulse points or in an oil burner. Rose or jasmine are good general essential oils and are close to the angelic vibration. The following are specific suggestions for each chakra:

🍃 Base — Patchouli, vetivert, myrrh.
🍃 Sacral — Sandalwood, jasmine, neroli, orange.
🍃 Solar — Juniper berry, vetivert, violet leaf, bergamot.
🍃 Heart — Rose, rose otto, lavender, geranium.
🍃 Throat — Roman chamomile, German chamomile, myrrh.
🍃 Third eye — Rosemary, juniper berry, clary sage.
🍃 Crown — Jasmine, rose otto, lavender, frankincense.

WORKING WITH PISTIS SOPHIA, THE HEAVENLY MOTHER

The true secret of inner peace, and a key part of the spiritual pathway, is to link with earth and sky and, through this, to connect to All Life as created.

The following exercise with Pistis Sophia will help you to achieve this connection. This builds on the exercise with Pistis Sophia in my previous book, *A Harmony of Angels*, and will enable you to bring in the energies of celestial star fire and sacred earth flame, which manifest as gold and silver, to balance your mind and body and unify as diamond within Spirit.

To benefit fully from this exercise, first practise sacred breathing. You do this by taking a sacred in-breath: breathe deeply through your nose, with your mouth closed and your tongue behind your upper teeth. For the sacred out-breath, move your tongue behind your lower teeth and breathe out with your mouth open. Once you have practised this for a few minutes it will seem quite natural.

🍂 Hold out your hands, palms up, on either side of you.

🍂 For this exercise remember that, when you connect to Source, usually it will be your left hand or foot that receives energy while your right hand/foot gives energy (although for a few people the flow will go the other way, i.e. left hand/foot gives and right hand/foot receives - this is still perfectly normal).

🍂 Now imagine that within yourself you are going to create the infinity symbol (as in the illustration of Pistis Sophia opposite).

🍂 Say the words, *"Pistis Sophia, Pistis Sophia, Pistis Sophia, please be with me now, in love and light, love and light, love and light."*

🍂 Say the words, *"Join my right hand through all that there is above, with celestial star fire to my left hand"*. As you do this, imagine that golden star fire extends in an arc from one hand to the other - you. may be able to feel the energy link being made by the golden (solar) ray of Source.

🍂 Now, "*Join my right foot through all that there is below, with sacred eternal flame to my left foot.*" As you do this, visualize silver earth flame extending from one foot through the very heart of earth to the other foot - you may feel the energy link being made by the silver (lunar) ray of Source.

🍂 Now say, "*Through my heart I am so joined*", and as in the illustration, the energy flow will cross and integrate into white-gold at your heart centre.

🍂 Feel this flow of energy and let your consciousness become part of it. In your heart is a spark of the Divine that wants to reconnect with all life.

🍂 When you are ready take a sacred in-breath and, while holding this breath, say mentally: "*Raphael, Raphael, Raphael, I breathe the love of Father Sun above into my heart, and I send it down to Mother Earth below*". On the sacred out-breath, will this golden energy down to Mother Earth.

🍂 Then take a second sacred in-breath. While holding this breath, say mentally: "*Gabriel, Gabriel, Gabriel, I breathe the love of Mother Earth below into my heart, and I send it up to Father Sun above*". On the sacred out-breath, will this silver energy up to Father Sun.

🍂 Then take a third and final sacred in-breath and, while holding this breath, say: "*Seraphiel, Seraphiel, Seraphiel, I breathe into my spirit the love of the father and the mother for me, the child of creation. I unify and magnify this love with the power of spirit and I send it to All Life*".

🍂 With the power of unconditional love and your own spirit you are unifying and magnifying the light of gold and silver, star fire and sacred flame into the crystalline diamond ray of Source.

🍂 As you breathe out this sacred breath of Unity you are one with All Life.

USING THE POWER OF SACRED SEVEN

Melchisadec is the ruler of the Sacred Seven planetary angels and guides your spirituality. He suggests that, if you wish to change or enhance your life so that you become more at peace with yourself, your first step could be to seek help from the Sacred Seven guardian angels. Invoke these angels, day by day, on their special days, and ask for loving support and assistance with their specific life focus.

You can also be aided by working with Hagith's sacred seven metals (one for each planet), for these are all part of the path to ancient truth and wisdom. Refer to the individual pages on each angel in the A-Z for messages from these angels to give you further guidance. Below, you will find the angel, planet, metal and focus for the seven days of the week.

🍂 *Monday*
Gabriel; Moon; silver or platinum. Hopes, dreams and aspirations.
🍂 *Tuesday*
Camael; Mars; iron. Courage, justice and forgiveness.
🍂 *Wednesday*
Michael; Mercury; mercury (as in a mirror). Strength, protection and truth.
🍂 *Thursday*
Zadkiel; Jupiter; tin. Abundance, wisdom and kindness.
🍂 *Friday*
Haniel; Venus; copper. Love, beauty and compassion.
🍂 *Saturday*
Cassiel; Saturn; lead (in pewter). Peace, harmony and serenity.
🍂 *Sunday*
Raphael; Sun; gold. Healing, energy science and knowledge.

OPENING THE HEART TO ACHIEVE UNIVERSAL HARMONY
This is an exercise that builds on the one for love and joy in my previously published box of *Angelic Abundance*. In this deeper version you are moving consciousness into your heart, from where you can be in permanent unity with the All, for once you open to unconditional love and compassion there is no more duality.

Green and aqua energy helps heal your personal heart chakra of past sadness, hurt or bitterness, allowing your higher heart chakra to open. Magenta is the colour of the higher heart, the heart of unconditional love, i.e. the ability to feel love and compassion for all life as created. This is the love of the Creator's angels, and when you open to this love you bring their joyful presence nearer to you. In this exercise to open the heart, you first bring in green and aqua energy of water of life. Then, seeing the heart as a six-petalled magenta flower (such as a rose or a lily), you bring in magenta energy that flows into the flower so it unfurls into incomparable beauty. Finally, you balance with gold and silver, and then the higher vibrations of gold, silver and the Tree of Life.

🍃 Invoke Metatron and Shekinah (Tree of Life) Raphael and Haniel (gold) and Gabriel and Phuel (silver) to be with you to aid you with this exercise, in love and light and for your highest good.
🍃 Breathe in deep breaths of white (positive) and breathe out negative (dark) emotions, until you feel filled with angelic energy, the breath of life and light.
🍃 Now take *nine* breaths (either normal or - for more power - sacred breaths)
🍃 Take the *first* in-breath and ask Phuel to bring green and aqua light down through your crown and into your heart centre.
🍃 As you breathe out, feel this soothing and calming energy flowing in, healing personal heart issues, ready to open your heart flower.
🍃 Ask Haniel to bring bright magenta light to pour into the flower of

your higher heart, petal by petal, as you take *the next six* breaths. With each in-breath, picture a loved one inside the petal for special healing. As you breathe out, see that petal glow with magenta light.

🪶 When all six petals glow with magenta light, pure, unconditional love and compassion is ignited within your heart and flows to and from each petal.

🪶 Take the *eighth* in-breath with Raphael, asking for the golden energy of creation to spiral down in an anti-clockwise direction from above, through the heart of the flower and around the petals of your heart. Then send it down to Shekinah (foot of the Tree of Life) to secure loving support for you in this earthly life; as you do this the gold turns white gold (a higher vibration).

🪶 Take the *ninth* in-breath with Gabriel, asking for the silver of creation to spiral up in a clockwise direction from Below, through the heart of the flower and around the petals of your heart. Then send it up to Metatron (crown of the Tree of Life) to guide your spiritual love in this life and complete your divine connection; as you do this the vibration changes it to white silver.

🪶 This is a point of unity and balance between masculine/feminine and physical/ spiritual aspects of self, and places you in universal harmony.

🪶 Your consciousness reaches out with infinite love towards the eternal Light.

🪶 Enjoy this wonderful feeling for a little while, sending love from your heart to all life, as well as to all the angels who were with you in the meditation.

Life needs and Angels

If there is any current situation for which you feel an angel could assist, you can speedily refer to this guide, which cross-refers to the A-Z of Angels in this book. For instance, if you are thinking of moving house, and would like to know which angel to consult, look up 'Moving house or country' and you will see that the angel is Nadiel. Refer then to the A-Z entry for Nadiel for more information.

Abundance: *Tubiel, Zadkiel*

Acceptance: *Ananchel*

Affirmations, colour: *Hahlii*

Air, healing power of: *Ariel*

Anger management: *Phaleg*

Animals, tame: *Hariel*

Animals, wild: *Thuriel*

April: *Tual*

Artistic inspiration: *Radueriel*

Aspirations: *Gabriel*

Astrology: *Umabiel*

August: *Hamaliel*

Beauty, general: *Haniel*

Beauty of self: *Haniel*

Beliefs: *Arad, Zadkiel*

Birds, tame: *Tubiel*

Birds, wild: *Anpiel*

Blue: *Michael, Zadkiel*

Broken heart, healing of: *Mupiel*

Caduceus: *Gabriel amd Raphael*

Calculating risks: *Barakiel*

Calming emotions: *Phuel*

Celestial secrets: *Raziel*

Change of direction: *Nadiel*

Choices: *Tabris*

Clarifying issues: *Ramiel*

Cleansing life: *Matriel, Torquaret*

Climax of a matter: *Amnediel*

Closure on a matter: *Geliel*

Colours, rainbow: *Hahlii*

Comfort: *Cassiel, Rachmiel*

Communication, verbal:
   Michael, Muriel

Communication, written:
   Dabriel

Compassion: *Cassiel, Rachmiel*

Confidence in leadership: *Verchiel*

Connection to earth/sky:
   Pistis Sophia

Copper: *Hagith, Haniel*

Cosmic Spirit: *Seraphiel*

Courage and confidence: *Camael*

Creativity: *Radueriel, Uriel*

Crown chakra: *Metatron*
Crown, above: *Seraphiel*
Crystals: *Och*

December: *Nadiel*
Decisions: *Zuriel*
De-clutter your life: *Tual*
Deliverance from a situation:
   Pedael
Depression: *Savatri*
Destiny, seeking: *Oriel*
Diamond ray: *Seraphiel*
Divine connection:
   Metatron/Shekinah
Dolphins: *Manakiel*
Door to Light: *Tabris*
Doves: *Alphun*
Dreams and hopes: *Gabriel*

Earth, healing power of: *Ariel*
Emotional calm: *Phuel*
Empowerment: *Camael*
Energy and wellbeing: *Mumiah*
Evaluating people or projects:
   Barakiel
Expansion of personal horizons:
   Adnachiel

Faithfulness and loyalty: *Icabel*
February: *Barakiel*
Feelings, voicing: *Michael, Muriel*
Fertility of body: *Yusamin*

Fertility of mind (new ideas):
   Yusamin
Financial affairs: *Vasariah*
Finding lost things: *Rochel*
Fire: *Uriel*
Fire of passion: *Nathaniel*
Flower secrets: *Achaiah, Anahita*
Food and nourishment: *Isda*
Forgiveness: *Camael, Phanuel*
Free will, choice: *Tabris*
Friday: *Haniel*
Future, harmony: *Isiaiel*

Goals in life: *Adnachiel, Gabriel,*
   Machidiel
Going with the flow: *Haurvatat*
Gold: *Hagith, Raphael*
Golden protection: *Diniel,*
   Kadmiel
Good luck (golden): *Diniel,*
   Kadmiel
Good luck (silver): *Aniel, Padiel*
Graceful acceptance: *Ananchel*
Green: *Haniel*
Grounding: *Gabriel, Pistis Sophia,*
   Raphael, Shekinah

Harmony: *Cassiel, Raphael*
Healing: *Raphael*
Healing of sun: *Raphael, Savatri*
Healing plants: *Anahita*
Healing the past: *Phanuel*

Health and wholeness: *Sofiel*
Heartbreak: *Mupiel*
Heart's desire: *Pagiel*
Heavenly peace: *Anafiel*
Hidden talents: *Parasiel*
Home/work balance: *Dokiel*
Home/work relationships:
    Hamaliel
Hopes and dreams: *Gabriel*
Hurts, healing of: *Matriel*

Ideas, new: *Spugliguel, Yusamin*
Inner feelings: *Muriel*
Innovation: *Uriel*
Insight: *Zikiel*
Inspiration, artistic: *Radueriel*
Inspiration, flash of: *Zikiel*
Inspiration, music: *Tagas*
Inspiration, poetry: *Israfel*
Intuitive problem-solving: *Ambriel*
Intuitive skills: *Cambiel, Ofaniel*
Invisibility: *Aniel, Padiel*
Iron: *Camael, Hagith*

January: *Cambiel*
Jobs and roles: *Jofiel*
Jobs, changing: *Nadiel*
Joy: *Haniel, Tubiel, Zadkiel*
Judgement, letting go of:
    Hadakiel
July: *Verchiel*
June: *Muriel*

Kindness and generosity: *Zadkiel*
Key to heavenly peace: *Anafiel*

Lead: *Cassiel, Hagith*
Leadership: *Verchiel*
Life partners: *Shekinah*
Life template, reprogramming:
    Pistis Sophia
Living your truth: *Michael*
Lost things: *Rochel*
Love, new: *Mupiel*
Love, power of: *Rikbiel*
Love, self-confidence: *Haniel*
Love, sexuality: *Amabiel*
Loving relationships: *Amabiel,*
    Haniel, Shekinah
Loyalty: *Icabel*

Magenta: *Haniel*
Magic of nature: *Aratron*
Managing time: *Eth*
March: *Machidiel*
May: *Ambriel*
Mercury: *Michael, Hagith*
Metals, power of: *Hagith*
Monday: *Gabriel*
Moon power: *Cambiel, Ofaniel,*
    Geniel, Amnediel, Adiel, Geliel
Mountains: *Rampel*
Moving house or country: *Nadiel*
Music and harmony: *Tagas*
Nature's magic: *Aratron*

Nature's plants and peace: *Sachluph*

Nature's secrets: *Achaiah*

Negative emotions, refocusing: *Phaleg*

New goals: *Machidiel*

New plans: *Adnachiel, Spugliguel*

New projects (calculation of risks): *Barakiel*

New projects commences: *Geniel*

November: *Adnachiel*

October: *Barakiel*

Opportunity for abundance: *Tubiel, Zadkiel*

Orange: *Uriel*

Passion for life: *Cassiel, Nathaniel*

Past: *Dabriel, Phanuel*

Patience: *Achaiah, Michael, Rampel*

Peace: *Anafiel, Cassiel, Duma, Seraphiel*

Peace with nature: *Rampel, Sachluph, Zuphlas*

Personal beliefs: *Arad*

Personal expansion: *Adnachiel*

Philosophy and wisdom: *Hermes Trismegistus*

Physical health and wellbeing: *Mumiah, Sofiel*

Pitfalls: *Zephon*

Pink: *Haniel*

Plants: *Anahita, Aratron, Sachluph*

Poetry: *Israfel*

Power of will and mind: *Gazardiel*

Prayer, power of: *Sandalphon*

Present: *Eth*

Principles: *Zadkiel*

Problem-solving: *Ambriel*

Protection, general: *Michael*

Psychic awareness: *Barakiel*

Psychic/spiritual development: *Ariel*

Purple: *Ariel*

Quiet reflection: *Duma*

Rain: *Matriel*

Rainbows, power of colours: *Hahlii*

Reach for the sky: *Sahaqiel*

Reconnect to earth and sky: *Pistis Sophia*

Recuperation and rest: *Farlas*

Red: *Camael*

Relationships: *Hamaliel, Haniel*

Relaunch your future: *Spugliguel*

Reprogramme life template: *Pistis Sophia*

Rest and recuperation: *Farlas*

Right job or role: *Jofiel*

River of life: *Haurvatat*
Root chakra: *Camael, Cassiel*

Sacral chakra: *Uriel*
Sacred flame: *Pistis Sophia*
Saturday: *Cassiel*
Sea mammals: *Manakel*
Secret wisdom: *Raziel, Hermes Trismegistus*
Self-belief: *Haniel, Pistis Sophia*
Sensitivity: *Barakiel*
September: *Zuriel*
Serenity: *Cassiel*
Sexuality: *Amabiel*
Silent reflection: *Duma*
Silver: *Gabriel, Hagith*
Silver protection: *Aniel, Padiel*
Simplify life: *Tual*
Sky: *Sahaqiel*
Sky's the limit: *Sahaqiel*
Solar chakra: *Raphael*
Song: *Tagas*
Source (healing): *Seraphiel*
Speaking your truth: *Michael*
Spiritual development: *Ariel, Melchisadec, Metatron*
Spiritual direction: *Melchisadec*
Star fire: *Pistis Sophia*
Strength: *Michael, Zeruch*
Sunday: *Raphael*
Sun's rays, power of: *Gazardiel, Savatri*

Taking stock: *Torquaret*
Third eye chakra: *Ariel, Melchisadec*
Throat chakra: *Michael, Zadkiel*
Thursday: *Zadkiel*
Time: *Eth*
Tin: *Hagith, Zadkiel*
Tuesday: *Camael*
Tranquillity: *Phuel*
Transformation: *Uriel*
Trees, peacefulness: *Zuphlas*
True love: *Amabiel*
True self: *Ithuriel*
Truth: *Michael*

Universal harmony: *Metatron/Shekinah*

Vigilance: *Zephon*
Violet: *Melchisadec*
Vision, power of: *Adnachiel*
Voicing inner feelings: *Muriel*

Washing away hurts: *Matriel*
Water, healing power of: *Phuel*
Wednesday: *Michael*
Wellbeing and energy: *Mumiah*
Whales: *Manakiel*
White-gold: *Shekinah*
White-silver: *Metatron*
Wholeness and health: *Sofiel*

Wild animals and birds: *Anpiel*,
    Thuriel
Willpower: *Gazardiel, Raphael*
Winding down situations: *Adiel*
Winds of change: *Ruhiel*
Wisdom, ancient: *Hermes*
    Trismegistus, Raziel
Wisdom, ancient and general:
    Zadkiel
Work/home balance: *Dokiel*
Work/home relationships:
    Hamaliel
Worries: *Iadiel*

Yellow: *Raphael*

FURTHER READING AND INFORMATION

Also by the author, published by Quadrille:

A Harmony of Angels (2001)

Harmony Angel Cards (2002)

Angelic Abundance (2003)

The author's website:

www.angelamcgerr.com

Other reference sites:

Angelic and Energy Healing and Products:

www.harmonyhealing.co.uk

Chakra notes, healing with music and sound:

www.soundsations.co.uk

Chakra essential oils information:

lav.moon@virgin.net

Suggested reading:

The Kybalion - Hermetic Philosophy

Crystal Healing, Vols. 1 and 2 - Katrina Raphaell

The Crystalline Transmission - Katrina Raphaell

Living in the Heart - Drunvalo Melchizedek

Edgar Cayce's Atlantis and Lemuria - Frank Joseph

The Gospel of the Essenes - Edmond Szekely

Genesis of the Grail Kings - Laurence Gardner

ACKNOWLEDGEMENTS

🪶 I should like to acknowledge, with a huge debt of thanks, the wonderful assistance that continues to be provided by everyone at my publishers, Quadrille. Particular mention must be made of the invaluable ideas, moral support and advice from my friend and editor, Anne Furniss (without whom these angel books and cards would probably never have happened) and the gifted graphic design input from Jim Smith. Also my undying gratitude to Richard Rockwood for providing yet more beautiful and inspired artworks.

I would also like to thank:

🪶 My husband Barry, and my children Fleur and Guy, who had to cope when my head was completely full of angels (and little else!)

🪶 My sister, Joanna, who started me on this learning curve, and without whose love and support on this path I would be bereft.

🪶 My sister Fiona, with whose gifts we shall extend the angelic concepts into spiritual gardens.

🪶 My friends Catherine Steer and Arya Ingvorsen, who provided constant encouragement and gave valuable feedback.

🪶 My friend and a source of great inspiration, Pat Arnold, who shared and corroborated information that was greatly beneficial.

🪶 Also, some assistance on this project came from new friends Gina Groom (student of the Cabbala and the angel Raziel) and Sharon Galliford (teacher of the wonderful healing possibilities of sound vibration).

🪶 And most of all, of course, I was lucky enough to receive the daily guidance of Seraphiel, Pistis Sophia, Michael, Melchisadec, Metatron and Shekinah. In addition, the others of the Sacred Seven (on their respective days of the week) and many other Gold and Silver Guardian Angels, who continue to show their unconditional love and support for us all, in the wonderful cause of Love and Light.

First published in 2004 by
Quadrille Publishing Limited
Alhambra House
27-31 Charing Cross Road
London WC2H OLS

Reprinted in 2004
10 9 8 7 6 5 4 3 2

Project editor: Anne Furniss
Senior designer: Jim Smith
Production: Beverley Richardson

British Library Cataloguing in Publication Data
A catalogue record for this book is available from the British Library

ISBN 1 84400 107 5
Printed in Hong Kong